**Cyberstalked and Deepfaked, Me Too!**
**Hijacked Minds. Protecting Yourself in** a Modern Sodom
**and Gomorrah.**

Introduction

I don't think people recognize how many things affect our minds. If you have been a victim, witnessed domestic violence, had a concussion, been in a car wreck, had chronic health problems, are overweight, have asthma, have parents who argued, tend to be impulsive, or have been bullied, your mind has been affected. Are you attached to SnapChat, Instagram, Facebook, pornography, or video games? Your mind has been affected.

Furthermore, if you have been prescribed medication or mood stabilizers for depression, anxiety, ADHD, and felt that it didn't help, didn't work or it worked the opposite, you're probably correct and your mind has been, in effect, hijacked. If you have had trauma in your past, your mind has been hijacked. If you smoke to feel calm or focused, your mind has been hijacked. If you need to drink alcohol to relax, become social, feel less stressed, you too, have been hijacked. If bread, cookies, cakes, or snacks call your name regularly, you too have been hijacked. If you have pain for no reason and need something to relieve that pain on a regular basis, your mind has been hijacked. If you take drugs to feel better, your mind has been hijacked.

This book may help you recognize how many of us have been living in distress and dis-ease, which leads to hijacked minds and then turns into DISEASE. Disease and disintegration come from hijacked minds and hijacked bodies. Let me help you reclaim the mind you were meant to have and lead the life you deserve.

Our bodies are starting to disintegrate at a much earlier age and at a faster rate than ever before in the last 100 years. What causes this disintegration? First of all, let's look at the meaning of disintegration from Webster's Dictionary. _1. To break or decompose into elements, parts, or small particles. 2. To destroy the unity or integrity of. 3. To_

1

Dana Shepard-Cardwell, M.Ed.

undergo a change in composition. Our minds and bodies are undergoing a change in composition. It's like moving forward with technology, the sedentary life, and fake food have taken us back to the dark ages. It's a modern-day plague.

Public Health.org shared that the average American ate 20% more calories in the last 20 years than they did 40 years ago. They noted that a rise in fast food sales correlated to a rise in body mass index and the lack of exercise has been a major culprit in the obesity epidemic and poor health factors.

Along with the disintegration of our bodies, *"one in five children have mental health problems. A 43% increase in ADHD has been noted. A 37% increase in adolescent depression has been noted. There has been a 200% increase in the suicide rate in children aged 10-14"* (Dr. Luis R. Marcos). Dr. Marcos, a psychiatrist, noted that our children today are being overstimulated (computers, TV, technology), over gifted, deprived of balanced nutrition and sleep, lack defined limits, lack movement and exercise outdoors, and don't get enough boredom in outdoor spaces to learn to self soothe and figure out problems by using their own creativity.

This book is for all walks of life. For females who need to keep *abreast* of what is going on right in front of their eyes. If you have Facebook, Instagram, or SnapChat, then this subject is a must. This topic also needs to be reviewed by males, if you have a computer and use it regularly. The particular and peculiar information provided in this book could discreetly save your relationship or even your freedom one day. Furthermore, if you are the parent of a male or female under the age of 20, you need to educate yourself before it's too late and help your children.

Why did I decide to address the matter of hijacked minds? Well, I too, have been hijacked one too many times and I finally had enough of "IT" when "IT" happened, again.

The Outre Day (violating convention)
I consider myself a strong, independent, active, yin/yang seeking feminist. I'm up to date on health topics and stay active. I've finished

Dana Shepard-Cardwell, M.Ed.

an Ironman race, seven marathons, a few obstacle races, many road races and numerous short triathlons. I was a probation officer and coach who could handle conflict when needed. I'm now a therapist and I specialize in working with clients who have trauma, addictions, anger issues, depression, PTSD, anxiety, and ADHD. I considered myself well-versed. Until....

On a bright beautiful Tuesday in August I awoke to find my studious husband on the phone. By this time, he had been up for over an hour and as I lumbered to the coffee pot, I picked up on some confusion in his voice. I gathered from the conversation that my strong-arm was included. As my husband and I may have commonalities related to our therapy clients, I figured this had to do with a referral. Au contraire. One syllable words were exiting my husband's mouth, "Oh", "Huh", "Uh", "Oh My". What in the world was he talking about and to whom? I remained fixated on my priority, at the moment, that black liquid gold with white vanilla flakes of sweet fantasy. (Pay attention to my choice of words.)

It was a bright sunny Tuesday when I woke up to find my diligent husband on the phone in what appeared a conversation that included my politically incorrect self. I assumed it was correlated to a client that we had in common. I focused on the warm tan liquid that was pouring into my cup. The summer was ending and I felt as if my cup was half full. A feeling of contentment filled up in my veins, until I slouched over my husband at his desk computer. Flabbergasted, I gasped for air.

It was a sullen Tuesday morning when I awoke to overhear my husband on the phone in a distressed manner. My main concern was the black and tan warm liquid substance as my cup runneth over and my husband expressed an overwhelming shock from his loins. I lumbered over to his computer finding my black liquid in projectile form exiting my pursed lips. "Damn it!" I exclaimed.

It was a blistering hot humid Tuesday in August when I awoke to find my husband wide-eyed and less than bushy tailed with a horrid look on his face and extremely startling photos which he gasped at on the computer. I hesitantly made my way over to him with my needed coffee fix filled with vanilla cream to see myself with two darker men

3

Dana Shepard-Cardwell, M.Ed.

servicing me at the same time in a very compromising position and blurted out "WTF?"

And that is how my stairway to hell nightmare started, over and over again... One hot sultry Tuesday in August.
"Seriously?", I thought as I hung up the phone that bright, sunny day in August. It was the end of a busy summer and the temperature was coming down from sultry to sensational. The birds were singing songs of love as they prepared for the fall. Who wouldn't be singing on a day like that?

I was finally at a place in life where my private practice was full and I was helping those with trauma move forward to lead productive and self-fulfilling lives. Ironically, as I hung up the phone, I just found out I had become a Victim, AGAIN! At age 50!! "What the hell is this world coming to?" I cried out in anger. I never thought I would be reliving this type of scene again, at middle age.

Sodom and Gomorrah were cities mentioned in the Bible, the Torah, and even the Quran. It is noted that Sodom and Gomorrah went up in flames, after God passed judgement on the cities. The cities were noted to be found on the Jordan River. Sodomy which came from the name of the ancient city is generally noted as anal or oral sex or even sex with an animal. The King James version of the Bible in Jude notes, "Even as Sodom and Gomorrah and the cities about them in like manner, giving themselves over to fornication, and going after strange flesh, are set forth for an example, suffering the vengeance of eternal fire." (Jude 1:7)

CNN reported (10/2019) that the number of US adolescents ages 12-17 admitted to emergency rooms for injuries related to sexual abuse doubled between 2010 and 2016! The study was published in JAMA Pediatrics and found an increase of more than 70% for child sexual abuse. More disturbing is that the study found there has been an increase in the number of young girls involved in human sex trafficking. (The study did find that it's not likely that all the increase in sexual abuse was correlated to human sex trafficking, but can account for some of the increase.)

4

Dana Shepard-Cardwell, M.Ed.

Don't think that video cameras and pornography aren't in play related to this increase in ER admissions, and although a girl may be abused by only a few perpetrators, her assault is often being recorded and sold on the internet. This plays into the sick, billion-dollar industry of pornography and the victimization of underage children. One doctor noted that most of the girls admitted to the ER for sexual assault don't disclose the nature of what happened to them in detail. This is how these demonic perpetrators work, they brainwash the girls, and have them so afraid that the girls stay quiet about what really happened.

To add insult to injury, one therapist, Amy Duffy, noted in her article *Counseling Survivors of Sexual Violence*, "One thing the mental health field has shown me is that helping sometimes requires us to combat the systemic and institutionalized injustices that are prevalent in our society. I recently found myself in a counseling session with a college-aged female who was displaying feelings of hopelessness and crying profusely asking me 'Why?'. She was directly asking me 'why' after her sexual assault and after exercising every legal right available to her, the system was failing her. Our society and our legal system have justice gaps that are expansive. I couldn't think of an answer I could provide in that moment that would address her feelings of hopelessness."

I too was up against Mt. Everest when I, and the other victims in town, filed our complaints and statements at the local police department. The male officer told us, "Well, I don't even know if an actual crime has been committed." If we were younger, we probably would have fallen through the cracks, but we aren't. We are educated, business owners who don't take injustice lying down on our backs while someone screws us from behind, from the front, sideways, upside down. Literally. If you saw the pictures involved, you would know I'm not exaggerating. We took our information to the local top notch detective, who happened to be female, at the sheriff's department, where the guy was already on probation.

One study found that more than 3.3 million American women ages 18-44 years old were raped the first time they had sexual intercourse. That's also true for my story. The average age of a rape victim was age 15 ½ and the average age of the perpetrator was 6 years older than the female. I was 17 and my perpetrator was 18/19. Most American women have been exposed to violence by age 24. My story of violence follows and the sexual assault is found later in this book.

Dana Shepard-Cardwell, M.Ed.

A Royal Pain in the Ass

Domestic violence is the leading cause of injury to women in the United States. (U.S. Surgeon General)

The website www.apa.org noted, "Violence and sexual violence against girls and women continue to occur with great frequency." They note a study (Kilpatrick et al, 2013) by the United Nations that indicated 70% of women experience some form of violence in their life; furthermore, they found around 90% of women in the U.S. have been subjected to this current statistic. The American Psychological Association notes that long term effects to child sexual abuse include: dissociation, anxiety, depression, substance abuse, suicidal ideations, eating disorders, and somatic issues (Briere & Jordan, 2009; Briere & Scott, 2014). Research continues to show that women who experience childhood trauma tend to be re-victimized later in life, also.

Sexual harassment is unwelcome sexual comments, advances, requests for sexual favors, or other verbal or physical conduct of a sexual nature. It generally results from someone who has power over another like a boss or teacher or coworker.

People who are sexually harassed may feel: angry, hurt, depressed, become easily distracted, unable to concentrate, feel trapped, suffer from physical ailments like stomach aches, headaches, or insomnia. Their self-esteem may begin to suffer with the lack of direct contact with others and less emphasis on their appearance like dressing down or gaining weight.

Ahh, the anger thing!! I think most of the clients I work with, from the residential treatment male teens, ages 11-17, to the females I see at my office all have anger issues, including myself. Once we have been victimized, which can include neglect during our upbringing, we tend to think with our primal brain at times and not our prefrontal cortex which makes decisions a bit more wisely than the primal, amygdala. I'll get to the brain later, just know if you have had any type of trauma in your life, you most likely have anger that surfaces like a massive volcano at times, and that is to be expected. Sit back, relax, read on, you're normal. Well, your reaction is normal, but your mind is hijacked!

Most people can visualize physical sexual harassment, but verbal

Dana Shepard-Cardwell, M.Ed.

harassment can also be jokes, remarks, teasing, comments about one's body or sexual activities, or a request for sexual favors. The best way to handle these situations is to talk to someone about it, keep documentation on the times and dates of the harassment, tell the person to stop, find out about policies on sexual harassment at your school or work place, and finally seek assistance if it continues.

Turns out the guy I was dating at 16, Jay, was similar to his bullying friends. What I did not know was that Jay's father had been abusing his mother and they were about to get a divorce. Jay had it all. He came from a wealthy family, they had a large home with a beautiful pool, a manicured lawn, tennis courts, and of course, a trampoline.

I remember going over to swim one afternoon. His parents left to run some errands. Jay and I jumped on the trampoline and then he started tickling me incessantly. I told him to stop tickling me and because he was such a sweet guy (said sarcastically), he said, "I'm going to tickle you until you pee in your pants." What was I thinking being with a loser like this? (Or is "IT" that he was just hurting?) We got in the pool after jumping on the trampoline and then playing some tennis where his goal was to "beat my pants off." Jay wasn't very good at tennis, so there was no beating my pants off.

In the pool Jay proceeded to tell me how the girl next door loved to come over and swim topless. She was our age, had been a cheerleader, got into drugs, dropped out of high school, and was touring the town with the bikers. Rumor was that she was a topless dancer. Age 16. Wow. What a great start in life. I said, "Sure, I'll be like Angie and swim topless." (Said sarcastically.) Not even close. Again, what was he thinking? It wasn't as if I was going to take my top off simply because his loser neighbor did. My guy friend pulled on my string bikini that was double-tied until it started to come untied.

I yelled at him, "TIE IT BACK!" He laughed and swam away. I swam to the side of the pool and tied the suit myself. I got out, upset and said, "I'm going home." I stormed out of the pool with an angry look on my face. Jay convinced me to stay and said he was sorry. He did the "poor me" route and said that he just needed someone to be with as his parents had been arguing a lot and he didn't want to be alone. I will say this: Guys are very intelligent when they think with their second head at this age. We, females, buy the "poor me" story

Dana Shepard-Cardwell, M.Ed.

and feel like we should take care of them. This is where hijacked minds start: from the abusers stand point realizing how to play on people and how the other person becomes hijacked by wanting to help and then being victimized. Why do we stay?

Jay asked me to come upstairs to his room to listen to some music he just bought.   Once up there, he tried to get intimate, I pushed him away. Jay then got into his drawer and pulled out a large bag of pills. Uppers, downers, speed, benzos, etc. I asked him, "Why do you have those?" He said it made him think better; it cleared his mind. He offered, I shook my head "No", and I preached. After a while, I yelled, "Are you crazy, you could end up taking too many of those things and killing yourself." I took the bag from him, walked over to the bathroom, and threw the pills in the toilet. I flushed them and watched those colorful little kaleidoscopes make their way down the pipe. It was a pretty sight in more than one way! So many of the colors of the rainbow swirling around in the toilet bowl. (By the way, I know now that is a "NO! NO!" don't flush pills or medication down the toilet or down the drain.)

Jay looked relieved that someone cared about him. I was mad and not wanting any part of his behavior. As a truce, he offered me a drink of Jack and Coke as he went downstairs to make it. He brought the drink back upstairs and I took a sip, but I ultimately didn't want to drink with him in the middle of the day. I asked Jay if he was afraid his parents would find out he was drinking in the home. He said they wouldn't even notice. I remember him going into his parent's room to get something. I decided this was a good time for me to leave, exited his room, and walked toward the steep staircase. Jay stopped me as I started to walk down the stairs.

I turned back to hear what Jay had to say. He asked if I trusted him. I told him, "I'm not sure." (Which was the truth.) He said he wanted to earn my trust back and would I play a game with him. "Depends on what it is." I told him. He asked that I grab his hand and lean back. I said, "NO!" He was trying some sort of tormented mind game. (And trying to see how far he could get with hijacking mine.)

Somehow he grabbed my hand, and then gave a little push, and there I went, tumbling down the steep stairs. I remember being in so much pain when I landed on the tile floor at the bottom, but not wanting to let on that he had hurt me. My pride was a big downfall. (Pun

Dana Shepard-Cardwell, M.Ed.

intended!) He half heartedly apologized. As if that wasn't enough, he started tickling me. Why? Probably because he was wanting to hurt me with the fall, and thought I wasn't hurt with my Academy Award performance. I have no idea what was going on in his tormented mind, but I was in serious pain trying to get his insensitive ass off the top of me.

He continued to wreak more havoc on me. Torture! As I drug myself out the door in a hurry, I headed to my car. Jay, the Royal Pain in my Ass, started spitting on me. Really, no lie, just spitting on and at me. What an idiot! I yelled to him as I was limping to my car, "You're an asshole and you need some therapy!"

I tried not to talk to him anymore, but a week later, I asked Jay what the hell he was doing on that day and why he would act like a two-year old. Jay said he was mad because I had been getting a ride from "Mike." Mike was a neighbor up the road from me who was 6-foot, 4-inches and a member of the basketball team. My car had been in the shop and Mike had been giving me a ride home from school earlier that week. What!?,,,,,all this abusive behavior because I was getting a ride home from a neighbor? I don't doubt the sexual tries were just for his gratification, but the tickling, pushing down the stairs, spitting, and pure meanness because I needed a ride? This guy had some serious issues and was already becoming like his abusive father.

Dr. Daniel Siegel in the developing mind series notes, "Avoidantly, attached children have been controlling and disliked by their peers." Furthermore, noting that if caregiver's unfavorable behavior doesn't change the child will withdraw from close relationships and become aloof. He also noted, "The release of stress hormones leads to excessive death of neurons in crucial pathways involving the neocortex and limbic system, the areas responsible for emotional regulation." (Siegel, D. 1999. The Developing Mind)

Cut those ties! "Stop the insanity!" There was an article in the Los Angeles newspaper (AP) about how exposure to violence in children affects their DNA. The article goes on to say "children who are exposed to violence experience wear and tear to their DNA that is similar to that seen in aging" furthermore, "they face a heightened risk of mental and physical disorders as adults."

Jay was already an angry teen who thought releasing his anger on an

9

innocent victim would help his plight. The only thing his anger got him was a drug problem and lack of intimacy, as far as I'm concerned. Turns out I chipped my coccyx (tailbone) that day. I could barely drive my Nissan stick shift.

I remember my mother asking me to run an errand. I told her that Jay was giving me a piggyback ride when we were on his tennis courts and I fell and injured my back. I wasn't about to go into the whole sordid details of all that happened with Jay. She wouldn't trust my judgment of guy friends and might become too protective. It's sad when a teen feels such lack of trust for anyone that they cannot talk about being physically abused. Communication is key. Parents, listen even when you don't want to hear "IT".

So, I told my Mom I was in pain. Mother said if I was in that much pain, I would have to give up my car for a while. (Her sarcasm matched Jay's at times.) I'm sorry, but I don't care what happened to you and how much pain you're in, telling a 16 year old to give up their car? No way. I ran the errand and continued to be in excruciating pain for at least a month. I had to drive lopsided because the side that got a small chip was so painful when I tried to shift gears or press the brakes. No wonder childbirth was a walk in the park for me!

It wasn't until six years later that I was in a minor —very minor car accident—which traumatized the chipped coccyx. The doctor said that as a result of the chip, I had grown a cyst in that area. The bump 6 years later during the fender-bender traumatized the cyst. I had to have surgery. Immediately. Let me tell you, they don't sew you up back there. "The stitches would come out when you sit down," the doctor told me. I had three feet of gauze stuffed into the wound for a week.

I passed out on several occasions standing up at home after the surgery. My first bath included getting my mother to help me in the tub. I felt helpless and re-victimized, again. I couldn't even look at the incision. It's humiliating to be in your 20's and have your mother help you bathe. I couldn't move my legs to get in or out of the car. I was a teacher and had to take time off from work. "IT" was completely frustrating. All the while, my mind is becoming deeply hijacked to react in the future in less than productive ways.

When I went back to have the gauze removed, I passed out when the

Dana Shepard-Cardwell, M.Ed.

doctor showed me the three feet that was stuffed inside my wound. No wonder my mobility was limited after the surgery. How can you move around with that much gauze stuffed in a little hole above your tailbone?

The chipped coccyx continued to cause trauma years later. Something happened a few years after the surgery, so I went to see a specialist. The pain started when I sat down on a bench and got this sting shooting up my spine. I was in another city at the time, San Antonio, teaching public school. My husband was a therapist at a hospital and did not get off until after 5 p.m. I was having issues with my tailbone and drove myself directly after school to see the specialist. What I didn't know was that the doctor was going to reopen my wound. He told me he was going to give me a local anesthetic and I wouldn't feel a thing. Having no idea he was sticking me with a knife, I felt an uncomfortable prick, then just some pulling. Nothing major. He told me what was going on back there and what he did should relieve the problem. I went to stand up and passed out in his office.

After coming back to consciousness, the doctor let me know he had to reopen the wound "slightly" and the pain must have caused me to faint. He told me he would give me a pain pill. I informed him that I could not take Demerol, Darvocet or Codeine, as it makes me feel violently ill. Doc said this was not any of those and that the Vicodin would work just fine. Mind you, I was in downtown San Antonio and had a 45 minute drive at rush hour back to my apartment. I trusted him, took the Vicodin, sat in the lobby for a while, did some deep breathing as suggested, and drank a glass of water. I was "somewhat fine" on the drive home, until thirty minutes into rush hour. I started to sweat profusely; my head started spinning. I thought I was going to puke and pass out at the same time. I pulled over into a parking lot, sat, and prayed for God to get me home safely. I was literally five minutes from home and trying to make it in one piece, not pass out, not wreck, and without getting sick all over myself and my car.

The Opioid Epidemic has occurred in three waves. The first wave began in 1991 when deaths involving opioids began to rise following a sharp increase in the prescribing of opioid and opioid-combination medications for the treatment of pain. The increase in opioid prescriptions was influenced by reassurances given to prescribers by pharmaceutical companies and medical societies claiming that the risk of addiction to prescription opioids was very low. During this time,

11

Dana Shepard-Cardwell, M.Ed.

pharmaceutical companies also began to promote the use of opioids in patients with non-cancer related pain even though there was a lack of data regarding the risks and benefits in these patients. By 1999, 86% of patients using opioids were using them for non-cancer pain. Communities where opioids were readily available and prescribed liberally were the first places to experience increased opioid abuse and diversion (the transfer of opioids from the individual for whom they were prescribed, to others, which is illegal).(https://www.poison.org/articles/opioid-epidemic-history-and-prescribing-patterns-182)

God saw me home safely that nightmarish day. I was miserable all night. It felt like I was going to pass out and throw up at the same time. I went to the toilet several times, but I can't recall if I ever threw up. Time passed and my wound got better, but there were times it swelled and caused me major discomfort. I ended up having a second surgery to remove all of the cyst 20+ years later. There were some rough years, though, all because a dysfunctional teenager with emotional scars had to make sure someone else suffered alongside of him.

Facts about domestic violence: Many batterers feel a need to control and tend to be looked at as possessive, controlling, and demanding. Often the cycle continues as they were victims of domestic violence themselves. The batterer may have poor impulse control and a short fuse, problems with controlling their temper. They may suffer from depression and be codependent on others in the family.

Dr. Shapiro notes in her book entitled *Eye Movement Desensitization and Reprocessing Therapy (EMDR)* that psychological trauma is associated with numerous changes in the nervous system caused by cortisol release which spikes adrenaline, causing fluctuations in neurotransmitters, and so forth, causing a loss of homeostasis in the body. This is one reason I use EMDR, along with mind and body work like yoga and meditation to help the person work through the imbalance that takes place after a small trauma or with Big Ts. Big traumas.

Furthermore, each one of us puts off some magnetic source of energy, the Hindus refer to it as prana, the Chinese as Qi (chi), and the ancient Greeks as vital energy. Research has shown that disturbances in the energy within our body creates an imbalance inside of us which leads

Dana Shepard-Cardwell, M.Ed.

to dis-ease, aka disease. Taking a pill or a handful of pills will never cure the imbalance of energy that happens after trauma. A pill will only work on a small transmitter that is part of millions of other transmitters flowing throughout our bodies.

When we target only one part of a pain from depression, anxiety, or somatic problems then we create a bigger imbalance, because we are not getting to the root of the problem. It's like a weed. When you pull up the top of the weed, it's roots are still there. Think of the Thistle weed. If you chop off the thistle, it will come back louder and stronger. Why take a prescribed pill to make things louder? You have only skimmed the surface and this may help for a short time, leading to other roots that will surface, along with the original problem coming back up.

Robert Whitaker in *Anatomy of an Epidemic* notes that many people in the 1990s "had suffered bad reactions to fluoxetine (aka Prozac) that a national Prozac Survivors Support Group had formed. Furthermore he reported, "the problem was that fluoxetine did, in fact, stir suicidal and violent thoughts in some people and during the summer of 1990, the issue of Prozac's safety burst into the news." Was my boyfriend at that time on Prozac? It makes me wonder; he was most likely depressed due to his parents' issues. I've seen many adolescents on anti-depressants actively attempt suicide or become violent after the medication was added, not prior.

A boy I have seen off and on for three years was switched from ADHD meds he had been on since 1st grade (he's in the 6th grade now) to a mood stabilizer. Within two weeks he was telling his parents that he wanted to die and was banging his head on the glass of the car. I recommended inpatient care due to this issue and a few others, but his mother took him back to his primary doc that day. The pediatrician told her that the boy's depression could get worse on mood stabilizers, but told her after the fact, not before. She was upset, rightfully so, that he didn't warn her of this ahead of time. This is a prime example of why primary care providers or pediatricians shouldn't play Russian roulette with mood stabilizers, anxiety meds, or antidepressants with children.

Back to my own trauma as a teen. My pain in the ass boyfriend who pushed me down the stairs that day was smoking weed on a regular basis. A new report by Meagan Brooks on Medscape.com (3/19)

Dana Shepard-Cardwell, M.Ed.

showed high potency cannabis has been tied to 50% of new psychosis cases. The study used 901 patients who had daily cannabis use and with first episode psychosis, along with 1,237 healthy matched controls who were not smoking cannabis. The study found daily cannabis users were 3x more likely to have first episode psychosis than those who didn't use cannabis. Perhaps he had a psychotic break that day?

On another note related to meds our teens are prescribed in the millions or thousands, Dr. Lauren Moran lead a study showing that some ADHD meds are tied to a higher psychosis risk than others. (Reported by Deborah Brauser 3/19 on Medscape.com) The reporter noted, "Amphetamines are associated with a higher psychosis risk than methylphenidate in young patients who take these agents to treat ADHD." She went on to note that, "Methylphenidate is the most frequently prescribed stimulant in many countries; however, amphetamines are the most prescribed ADHD meds in the US." Among the young patients who participated in the study the risk for psychosis was almost twice as high with those who took amphetamines within the first 4-5 months as compared to those who took methylphenidate. So, which drugs have amphetamines? Adderall is the top stimulant with amphetamines. Methylphenidates tend to be your Ritalin, Concerta, and Daytrana products. Adderall tends to be a favorite for adults and college students with ADHD, it just may not be the best for the developing young mind. Maybe a psychotic break related to ADHD meds was the cause of me being pushed down a flight of stairs that day. Perhaps it was that and all the weed he was smoking, the alcohol, and the pills he took? I guess I'll never know. Seems like he was brewing up a recipe for disaster, only it affected me more than him.

If you look at history, psychiatric drugs were not prescribed to children and teens prior to the 1980s. Now we have approximately 6.0% of U.S. adolescents aged 12–19 reported to be involved with psychotropic drug use in any given month. Anyone thinking, "Are our kids, girls especially, being victimized by Western medicine even before they become a statistic to violence?" Refer back to the statistic I shared that 90% of U.S. women will experience violence in their lifetime.

This is my main emphasis. I'm not against Western meds and prescriptions. I just know that many times a doctor spends 10 minutes

Dana Shepard-Cardwell, M.Ed.

with a patient, and as a doctor, he or she thinks they have the magic bullet, and prescribes a powerful drug that could end up doing more harm than help.

To add to the fire, the APA cites numerous studies that point to the fact that social media and unemployment affects females at a larger percentage through their lifespan than males, which in turn, accounts for many depression diagnoses. Too many times social media portrays females as sex objects. Resulting in low self esteem for girls or reasons for them to feel they should modify their body in some form or fashion and act in a sexually explicit manner due to requests from males or portrayals they see in magazines or on TV. As a result, these girls become depressed or anxious, go to their primary care doctors, and become zombies from their depression meds or anxiety meds.

After another trauma I experienced years later with my daughter almost dying from pneumonia related issues as a baby and getting one medication after another, which didn't help her, I have little faith in our current Western medical system. As it turns out, she had a low tolerance for gluten which would sit in her tummy and rot and food particles would aspirate into her lungs. Food and lungs don't mix. She had five specialists: a pediatric gastroenterologist, a pediatric pulmonologist, a pediatric cardiologist, a pediatrician, and a chiropractor for pediatrics. Not one doctor concluded it was gluten issues. She was tested for celiac disease, but the test picks up on full blown gluten allergies, not intolerances.

It wasn't until I took her to a nutritionist/dietician that he noted that her symptoms seemed to be related to gluten, but that wasn't until she was five and had undergone eight different week-long stays hooked up to IVs in hospitals. She became so afraid of needles, that later as a teen, she passed out just getting a shot. Her depression and anxiety increased at puberty. What she endured as a baby and young child was directly related to hospital stays with many nurses trying over and over to find a vein to start an IV. This, in and of itself was traumatic for her and myself.

How does therapy help? Dr. Shapiro noted that during the bilateral stimulation of EMDR therapy, working memory is taxed which stimulates the orienting reflex and an associated parasympathetic response takes place, along with similar processes that characterize rapid eye movement (REM) sleep. In fact, I have had quite a few

Dana Shepard-Cardwell, M.Ed.

teens actually fall asleep or end up in a trance-like state during the bilateral eye movement stage of EMDR. It's just an amazing process watching angry or confused teens work through past disturbances and then walk out calm as cucumbers or as peaceful as penguins after several EMDR sessions.

Back to batterers and violence, on the opposite spectrum, the batterer may be narcissistic, where everything revolves around him or her, displaying an exaggerated ego and sense of extreme self-importance. Think of a political figure where they were so full of themselves on every news channel or Tweet. Many batterers have low self-esteem and are insecure, yet come off looking jealous and defensive.

Batterers may rationalize that violence is their way of dealing with pent-up feelings. However, no person should deal with their feelings by becoming violent toward themselves or others. Therapy is needed to break the chain of domestic violence and teach victims to become survivors, not just another statistic. We need to be able to love ourselves before we can attempt to love others.

It's sad, but true, that too many teens think that if they have a child they can love, the child will make up for the love they never received. This irrational thought is so far from the truth, and I pray that teens in domestic violence situations will reach out for help and counseling. The U.S. Department of Justice estimates that 95% of the victims of domestic violence are women. Out of emergency room visits, it is said that 35% are a result of domestic violence, and to add fuel to the fire of those who abuse their partner, over 65% also physically and/or sexually abuse the children in the home. (The Federal Bureau of Investigation) *Iron Nugget: Have you had an experience with violence?*

Dana Shepard-Cardwell, M.Ed.

Releasing the TIE that Binds You

What is *your* pain? We all have some sort of pain at some time in our lives. One of my "pains" came from listening to doctors who didn't know much about anti-depressants. What can you teach others about your pain? Most of us can take pain and turn it into a learning experience to help others. Personally, my mission is to help others find natural ways to heal themselves, before jumping into the pharmaceutical world of psychotropic medication, that tends to be a rollercoaster ride that you may not be able to come off.

Some of you will take your pain from the past or present and use it to help others, while another group will focus on their pain and complain about it. Resilience is 90% mental and 10% physical. I tell male teens who want to become Navy Seals that if they have the 90% mental drive to strengthen their resilience muscles then the 10% physical will follow with proper training. It's like body building or doing the Ironman race, one must train their muscles to get them where they want to go. The same is true with your mind. You must strengthen your mind to get what you want, not ignore the past and complain about it. That will only help your mind atrophy or increase in anger and distress. Anger comes from fear. Are you feeding the fear and anger monster or becoming resilient and using positive coping tools to help yourself and others?

Negative cognitions like, "I can't handle it" lead to anger, sadness, disappointment of self or others. Trauma may cause an imbalance in many of our neurotransmitters such as dopamine, serotonin, GABA, or norepinephrine. Between low neurotransmitters and negative cognitions, we become out of balance and may be easily startled, easily angered, cry frequently, have trouble sleeping or concentrating, develop constipation or IBS, get diarrhea with a nervous stomach (anxiety), become easily tired, have hypoglycemia, not able to focus at work or school, turn to drugs or alcohol, have little interest in sex, or too much interest in sex feeling like that's the only way to attach to others. Regardless, trauma will affect your mind.

Iron Nugget: A study listed in Prevention Magazine cited *The American Journal of Clinical Nutrition* found a cup of blueberries a day helped adults with metabolic syndrome which included excess belly fat, high blood pressure, and high blood sugar. It's amazing how Americans make excuses for healthy sugar and note they can't eat

17

Dana Shepard-Cardwell, M.Ed.

fruit because it raises their blood sugar, yet they will eat pounds of processed foods made with white or wheat flour, which sends the blood sugar to Mars and back. Blueberries have antioxidants which help your body become stronger and healthier and feed your brain anthocyanins. I usually add a handful of blueberries to my smoothie, along with bananas and walnuts. I'll address that later. Come to think of it, after reading this study, I think I'll increase the amount of blueberries,.

The energy that goes IN, determines what comes OUT. So, why do I have issues with Western medicine? I'll give the short synopsis. My daughter Cami was born with serious health issues related to asthma and numerous hospital bouts of pneumonia. She almost died, turning blue on one event. I was so afraid of losing her that I lived in fear, anger, and depression for those first five years of her life. I got down on my knees one day, after earlier cursing God and eventually agreed to allow God to take the wheel. (Jesus Take the Wheel was one of her favorite songs.) God allowed me to find the direction I needed by taking some of her medical problems in my own hands, since five specialists had done nothing but drug-up my child by age 5 and nothing was changing. I studied, I learned, I changed, and she got better. It took a long time.

Food IS Medicine. You can fill your body with processed garbage, but you will get mood and health problems sooner rather than later. My daughter is a prime example in her young years. By the way, macaroni and cheese was her favorite. I would get her to eat broccoli by allowing her to eat processed noodles, which were destroying her gut and immune system. Then her regular macaroni stopped at age 5, and bribing her to eat broccoli became harder!

For adults, slim your waist to improve your mood and protect your brain. Keeping our middle section from growing will help us feel better emotionally and help us live longer, physically. Try natural herbs like turmeric, ginger, cayenne, to add to lemon water with local honey. This detox water will help if you drink a glass upon first waking, during the day, and prior to going to sleep at night. Make a batch every few days in a big jug to keep in the fridge and then take 52-64ozs daily. You might want to boil some green tea, add the herbs, then the honey and lemons, and refrigerate as a nice green tea. Don't boil the honey or lemons.

Dana Shepard-Cardwell, M.Ed.

Why Hurt People Hurt People

Before we get into why hurt people, hurt other people, I need to distinguish the difference in a hurt person and sociopath or psychopath in layman's terms (antisocial personality disorder). A psychopath tends to feel entitled and tends to lack empathy for their actions. A hurt person more than likely has a conscience and a self-regulator that tells them what he/she has done is wrong. A psychopath will not have a self-governing moral compass. There is something missing in that part of the brain.

In Anna Salter's book, "Predators" she goes into detail how a "Persuasive predator" and a "power predator" work. The more common predator being the persuasive predator. Think about the person who "grooms" their victim through manipulation. He or she takes time to invest in the victim and then zeroes in for his or her prey. (Pay attention to this description to be used later in this book.) A psychopath will blame the victim or other reasons on his/her guilt. Ms. Slater notes that about 60% of psychopath sex offenders would still reoffend even after the most effective treatment available today.

I have one client who worked on her trauma of being groomed by a predator when she was almost a teen, being raped, given alcohol and cigarettes, and then getting pregnant and being so scared, so humiliated, so ashamed. The perp took her to get an abortion and she was not even legally a teen. Then he ditched her for another teen her age. That's a messed up persuasive predator!

I have helped many abused women I see in therapy who were groomed, raped, abused, and got pregnant and then got abortions at a young age. From low socio-economic girls, to middle class, to high society females. This is a problem folks. Along with these issues, I see women who contract Herpes from their sexually deviant partners. It's a plague. So many women from teens to their 30s have been affected by this life altering disease. You need to open your eyes if you are single!! Many of the people you see in your daily journey are suffering in silence from herpes. Don't assume the person you are flittering with is unaffected!

One of my favorite modalities in therapy when working with delinquent populations is Reality Therapy developed in the 1960s by psychiatrist, Dr. William Glasser. Dr. Glasser shows approaches to

19

Dana Shepard-Cardwell, M.Ed.

use in handling a problem of behavior. Basically, "Everyone who needs psychiatric treatment suffers from one inadequacy" and that is the person is "unable to fulfill his/her essential needs" (Glasser, 1965). I think of it more as an attachment issue. It can be a lack of ability to attach to people, but then it can also be food, or material objects that a person feels they are unable to fill the need of.

With delinquent teens, I support Glasser's take that it is not enough to help the teens face reality, but also to help them figure out ways to fulfill their needs if they are to live a crime free and fulfilled life. In the case of hurt people "therapy will be successful when they are able to give up denying the world and recognize that reality not only exists, but that they must fulfill their needs within its framework" (Glasser, 1965). Basically, to live within the construct of society's rules and boundaries.

Too many examples support the idea that hurt people "try desperately in many unrealistic ways to fulfill their needs" (Glasser, 1965). This is where a good therapist comes in to play a part in the hurt person's healing. A hurt person must become actively involved with at least one person in a better way than he/she is now or they will be unable to fulfill their needs. "Well-meaning advice always fails, patients can't straighten up and fly right when someone points out reality to them when there is not sufficient involvement" (Glasser, 1965). The point is this, just talking to any therapist who nods their head, won't work.

As a therapist, I get right into the nitty-gritty with my clients. I use numerous types of therapy from Reality therapy, cognitive behavior, EMDR (eye movement desensitization and reprocessing), Mindfulness, breathing and even yoga. I saw how Mindfulness and yoga improved my own life years ago, and as a result, I became a certified yoga instructor to use in my private practice with at-risk, depressed, anxious, and traumatized clients.

The basis of Reality Therapy is "helping patients fulfill two basic psychological needs: the need to love and be loved and the need to feel that we are worthwhile to ourselves and to others" (Glasser, 1965). By now, you should have picked up on the fact that "rule breakers" are very different than serial killers or serial rapists.

Dana Shepard-Cardwell, M.Ed.

My goal is to help you see the difference. With a rule breaker, we just
need to point that person in the right direction to get the help they
need. On the opposite spectrum with psychopaths, true beasts, who,
no matter what modality or what direction you point them in, just
have not shown the ability to change. It is You who needs to change
your course and sail off as far away from this beast as possible. Don't
stay in a catastrophic relationship, you are only hurting yourself and
those around you.

Recognize that with the "pit bull" or those who are hurting, Glasser
points out that we all have the same needs, but vary in our ways that
we can fulfill them. To be successful in life and in relationships one
must love others and allow ourselves to be loved back. It's not just
one or the other thing, it needs to be both. We must be able to give
and receive love. Think of the person at Christmas who only wants to
give or to receive. Chances are there is something a little off about
that person. The same in life we can't just give and not receive nor
can we just take and not give back.

The book "Predators" goes on to note that most psychopaths can lie
even when smiling and looking you straight in the eye. Their tactics
include "the ability to charm, to be likeable, to radiate sincerity, and
truthfulness." The idea that a predator comes from a lower socio-
economic status or bad home is totally false and researchers are still
figuring out a commonality between those diagnosed with predator
type behaviors. Some research has recently suggested a deviation in
the limbic system of predators in jail and that there seems to be a
missing link in the brain which regulates between what is right and
what is wrong.

In Ms. Salter's book Gavin de Becker noted, "Research has shown
that boyfriends or stepfathers are much more likely to abuse their
partner's child than the child's biological father." I've seen this
example in too many cases with the teens I counsel. And many times,
the mother will be at work or asleep when perversion takes place.
"Secrecy is the lifeblood of sexual aggression" (Salter, 2003).

A statistic to remind yourself on how serious sexual assaults are,
around 1 in 3 females have been sexually assaulted versus about 1 in
6 males. (According to the National Intimate Partner and Sexual
Violence Survey, 2012) This adds up to around 25% of our U.S.
female population. Furthermore, most studies report 50% of U.S.

Dana Shepard-Cardwell, M.Ed.

females have been involved in at least one violent situation. That is too many to remain quiet for any longer.

The time is now to recognize the difference between a psychopath and a hurt person who needs help. We can break the cycle of hurt people, hurting people, but not so much in the case of a psychopath which is another "animal" in and of itself. In other words, when you see a rattlesnake, run the other way, and call the local authorities to cage the viper. A pit bull on the other hand, may just need some retraining to get back on track and appropriate direction to become acclimated into a loving home.

I suspect some of you are in a relationship where it seems like all you do is give and the other person has a problem giving back or habitually takes. My case in point. "When we are unable to fulfill one or both of our needs, we feel pain or discomfort in some form" (Glasser, 1965). Glasser goes on to note that those who have problems showing love or giving love may stem from being afraid of rejection. As in the case of many teen delinquents, they have never been shown appropriate love and thus have a hard time giving love due to inappropriate role modeling. Many of them have fears of rejection as their most primal needs were never met. It only makes sense they lash out at others and continue to lack real attachment with reality and with others.

I try to help those who have been hurt decide what it is about his or her behavior that fails to meet his needs and then help them become committed to try another positive behavior, which will meet those needs while becoming more acceptable in reality as correlated to the morals and standards of life. A person must become motivated to change his behavior as he or she can't live another person's life and be healed at the same time. I tell clients if they ask me what I think they should do in a situation, "I don't know; what works for me won't necessarily work for you. You have to figure out what works for you to be successful. I'll give you some tools for you to put in your tool box, but you need to figure out what tool works best for you."

Iron Nugget: What positive things do you fill your tool box up with?

Back to my surprise on that beautiful, sunny August day. I knew finding myself as a porn star on a website was not currently working

Dana Shepard-Cardwell, M.Ed.

for me and someone must pay the price. My name was splashed all over the site as "Dana, the MILF". You can fill in the acronyms.

Glasser points out how important it is for learning to fulfill our needs to start early in life as "when we fail to learn we will suffer and this suffering drives us to try unrealistic means to fulfill our needs." Think of the woman who is overly materialistic, always shopping, or the man who drives the top of the line power truck or sports car that sets him above the others in his class. You know when these people drive up or walk into the room. There's almost a silent magnetism that has turned your head to look their way, along with almost everyone else in the room who watches that person as they enter. The problem is, these people fill needs in unhealthy ways through power, control, admiration, but none of that is real. Just because you turn your head to look at me when I enter the room, doesn't give me my hijacked mind back. Those people have hijacked minds and they probably don't even know it.

On the other end of the spectrum, Daniel Siegel, MD in his piece "The Developing Mind" supports my Jedi Mind trick I use with clients. Dr. Siegel shares examples of a good therapist in tune with their client. He talks about a nonverbal attuned form of communication called "affect attunement".

The part that I use with clients is related to "the brain of one person and that of another influencing each other in a form called co-regulation." Furthermore, he notes, "This is the fundamental way in which the brain activity of one person directly influences the activity of the other." I agree, totally, and share his ideas with clients that our collaborative communication allows our minds to connect with each other. The question is, "Is your mind open to being connected, or are you so stuck that your walls won't allow penetration of the healing kind?"

Some minds are so focused on healing that those people have been studied and were able to heal their own cancer cells. Then, there are some people who can get you to like them no matter what is going on with you because of their strong, connected minds to your inner soul or your inner child. Wouldn't it be nice to allow your EGO to be set aside for a while and just allow yourself to be healed?

23

Dana Shepard-Cardwell, M.Ed.

Recognize that we have a tendency to repeat behaviors unless we make a conscious effort to alter it in some way. The same choices, the same results. This is the danger of autopilot. As I finish this book, I'm on a solo cruise to Key West and the Bahamas. I needed to break away from my daily routine and the gibberish with my husband at night that keeps me on autopilot. Do you continue to remain miserable in life and in relationships? You may want to turn the looking glass inward instead of looking outward and blaming others. If your job is highly stressful, maybe you should look for another one or take vacation time, but staying miserable only hurts you and those around you.

This summer my husband and I took a cruise with another couple. The woman was miserable because she hated her current teaching job, she complained at dinner one night because she said she had put in many applications to other schools, but no one was calling her. She played the victim role saying her husband wouldn't support her in not working. I was trying to help her and became the butt of her anger. What I was thinking in my mind…this is the same woman who raised her children at home for many years and home schooled them. In fact, she took on several nanny type jobs in her home, while raising her son, one being my child and another child, where she was paid for her time. As for me, I have never been able to not work, except the three months after my daughter was born. I didn't remind her of this, but I did try to help her reframe her negativity to point out that when I, too, was miserable in teaching and didn't get any call backs from other schools, I had to ask myself, "How bad do I want to leave teaching?" When I tried to share this, she raised her voice at me started crying, and told me she never wanted to do massage or the things that I did back then (personal training, massage, permanent cosmetics). Then she got up and left the room when the dinner had just been served.

I was shocked! I'd been attacked. I was just trying to support this woman and help. This is what I got? What I wanted to share with her is that I never, ever, thought I would want to be a massage therapist. I liked getting massages, just as she did, but I was grossed out by feet, smelly feet, clean feet, you name it. I didn't want to work on feet or people with acne on their backs! This is not a joke! However, because I had to weigh the odds of staying in a sexist teaching job, where the environment was rife with nepotism, or leave teaching altogether. I needed to look at a field that would afford me the same yearly earnings as teaching with as little time invested as possible. Looking

Dana Shepard-Cardwell, M.Ed.

around I found that massage school would take 6-9 month and cost $3,000. Personal training took less time and less money, and permanent cosmetics the same as personal training. This became my plan to make a living without the demeaning and demanding stress of teaching and coaching.

What I did share with "my friend" is that God has a way of working things out through prayer, yet she went off on that, too, saying I was judging her. I wasn't, this is the truth for me. God had a way of allowing me to see that massage took my overthinking, over-stimulated brain off-line while I was working. I sensed what was going on with my clients through my hands and my quiet mind. Back when I did massage, it was the first time in my life that I became grounded. I recognized how important breath and calming the mind worked. My massage clients grew to love me as their therapist (I had a Hollywood producer as a client and a top politician's wife) and I grew grounded and peaceful. It was a win-win situation. Plus, I made the same salary, if not more, than I did as teaching with less stress. Calm music became my thing and working intuitively became the new ME. I had arrived, by chance!

"Sometimes you have to let go of the picture of what you thought life would be like and learn to find joy in the story you're living" (Mental Health Prime). Ironically, this message was posted by a woman I went to High School with who had terminal cancer and died on my birthday two weeks after she posted this saying. If that's not foreshadowing for the rest of us, I don't know what is.

Glasser notes we should pay attention to responsibility. When we act in such a way as to not deprive others of their need to fulfill love then we are acting in a responsible way and improving our own needs of self worth. A person who sabotages your needs is deep down only sabotaging their own self worth, it's a no win situation. "People do not act irresponsibly because they are ill; they are ill because they act irresponsibly" (Glasser, 1965). This is a heavy statement to contemplate, but a true gem to live by in helping hurt people heal.

Regarding my porn related perpetrator, I started wondering what was wrong with the person who did this to me. There were almost 100 photos of my face pasted on to women in lewd sexual acts. It must have taken some time to do this. This was scary. Not only was I victimized, but there were pictures of my High School daughter in her

Dana Shepard-Cardwell, M.Ed.

cheer uniform on the website as well. The cheer uniform could identify where she went to school. There was more than one picture of her. In fact, there were many more pictures with the two of us together. Those pics weren't altered. Granted those pictures had us clothed, but they were mixed in with fake nude photos of me and advertisements for porn. The advertisements were video shots of women giving oral sex to men or men masturbating. Some advertisements had women getting semen sprayed on their face.

Folks, it's simple, this life has good and evil. Our mission should be to align ourselves with healthy, honest, and good connections. It's not that evil will always be toxic. Some will recognize they've strayed off their path and they will correct their journey and get back on a good, solid footing.

I feel this is the case with many of the abused, aggressive teens I work with. I tell them the adults in their lives go astray by neglecting and/ or abusing them, but it may not be this way forever. I help them process that their drug addicted parent may one day get the help they need. This is where prayer and forgiveness come in. We can only control our own lives, but we can pray for others and forgive them for their transgressions.

Church and yoga bring connectedness to others. Yoga teaches us to live in the moment and in such a way that we cause no harm in thought, speech, or action to any living being....Wait for it.... Including ourselves. This is the first and foremost of the five yamas in the Yoga Sutra. Proverbs 4 reminds us to guard your heart at all costs, for it determines the course of your life. "Keep your mind free of perversity, keep corrupt talk from your lips. Let your eyes look straight ahead. Give careful thought to the paths for your feet and be steadfast in all your ways. Do not turn to the right or left; keep your foot from evil."

It's pretty simple, some of the TV shows, social media, alcohol, drugs, porn, immortality (lust and sexual pervasiveness) lead people to get their feet stuck in the evil muck. It's messy, sticky, smells bad, and doesn't easily wash off. The funny thing is, we see it on the guilty, but they hardly see it on their own bodies. If we aren't careful, we'll step in what they brought in and it will get on our shoes, hands, face, all over us, too.

When dealing with hurt people, Glasser notes, "In their unsuccessful effort to fulfill their needs, no matter what behavior they choose, all patients have a common characteristic: They all deny the reality of the world around them." He goes on to say that the therapist that accepts the patient's excuses or allows the patient to ignore reality, for example, or who allows the patient to blame his unhappiness on a parent or on an emotional disturbance can usually make his patient feel good temporarily, but at the price of evading responsibility and leaves the patient feeling disillusioned and ultimately unsuccessful in therapy, and unsuccessful in life.

I recently met with the ex-husband of a "friend" who I wrote about in my first book, who deeply hurt me and I felt was rather "toxic" to be around. When I met with her ex it was to give him a copy of the book as he had been recently deeply hurt by her, also. She had spread rumors around town that he was abusive. (This is what he told me as I don't speak with her anymore, since I wrote that book and she and all her groupies shunned me.) Our meeting was not to gang up on her, but to talk about our own pain we received and to recognize that some people even with mental health intervention either choose not to change or may not be capable of changing. He talked about how he prays for her to be blessed and happy everyday as she is still the mother of his children.

This guy takes forgiveness to the next level. I even told him, "Wow, that's amazing. I'm not sure I could do that." He noted it is hard some days to forgive her and want the best for her, after the things she has done, but he knows in his heart it's what God wants. (or something like that). The very next day after we met, a Facebook memory popped-up on my page of his ex-wife with me and the other two ladies we did Ironman with. I think that was the only picture we all took together and I was flabbergasted at the irony. I sent him the picture and noted how ironic it was as we just talked about how it was 8 years since Ironman and there are very few pictures with his wife.

This is his reply to my message: "I am not a big believer in irony or coincidence. I believe that you are being invited by Jesus to be set free from wounds. I believe we are given these opportunities in the Spirit we can partner with resentment (the enemy) or forgiveness/gratitude (Jesus). I believe you, Eric and I are being invited to walk out of these chains and pray for (his ex) and (her BF) and the past to be healed and forgiven. That God blesses them with

27

Dana Shepard-Cardwell, M.Ed.

every good thing that we hope to receive for ourselves. So in summary, it's not irony, it's an offer and an opportunity in the Spirit. A window that is open now, but only for a season. Pray about it. I am." I'm telling you this guy should be a Christian therapist. He's got the anointing!

As a therapist, I can't beat appropriate choices into my client. A client needs to have an investment in changing old/bad habits to heal or to get better. Think of AA, the client must first admit they have a drinking problem before working through their steps to recovery. And one of the steps to healing is making amends with those they have hurt. In the past, the ex-wife of a friend would look like she was getting help for her issues, but he pointed out that she didn't seem to be cleaning her side of the street. She continued to worry about the other side of the street, meaning she would point out the problems of other people and continued to run from her own, literally. She is a good athlete and she would put 90% of her time and effort into running events or triathlons.

This is the part of therapy that sometimes has therapists looking like the obstacle. Therapy is not about putting band-aides on your wounds. It's about getting rid of the deep embedded wart that eats away at your skin and sooner or later becomes a cancer on your heart, soul, and mind. You want to remove this obstacle, not put a little ointment on it and cover it up when it's still there. A therapist who just listens and says, "Oh that must have been so painful. It was so horrible what you went through." helps with only a piece of the puzzle, and may not allow you to see the whole picture. You want to remove that wart to live a wonderful and mindfully healing life. There will be more bumps and bruises, but removing the obstacles from your earlier life will help you. And when speed bumps come up in the future, they will be so much easier to maneuver this time and make your way around them.

Dana Shepard-Cardwell, M.Ed.

PTSD

If you can't reflect upon yourself, therapy won't be done. When we are stuck in the feelings/emotions state (Amygdala) the PFC (prefrontal cortex) is off-line and lacks the ability to make executive decisions (planning, working memory to follow through on tasks or directions, flexibility going from Plan A to Plan B to Plan C, self-control, focus, having issues with impulsivity, lacking thought process of why others may do what they do, interpreting things).

After trauma, Dr. Bessel van der Kolk (The Body Keeps the Score) pointed out that people are not comfortable in their own skin. When traumatized, we react differently than those not traumatized. Bessel found yoga and nonverbal tools used by trainers helped to get people comfortable in their own body and skin. He emphasized, this should be number one when working with traumatized patients.

Clinicians and doctors, i.e. society, have it backwards!! Therapists rush in because they are ready, but the client is NOT! Doctors rush to prescribe a one pill fits all, which leads to another pill, then another pill, and so on. Then what happens is the patient starts wondering, "What's wrong with me? Why is this not working?" Sooner or later the patient becomes even more distressed, even more traumatized, and resorts to all sorts of negative tools and later asks, "Am I crazy?"

I shout at the American Psychotropic Medical Model. That is what's wrong, that's what's crazy. The model for helping the traumatized. It's the way society thinks we should do therapy and medication, first. No, my friend. We need to treat the body first to fix the MIND! Yoga and Mindfulness should be our first resort, along with appropriate massage therapy. Then, and only then, once

29

Dana Shepard-Cardwell, M.Ed.

the body is addressed and calm, the trauma work with talk therapy can begin.

One of my client's who wrote about her drug, rape, and human trafficking ordeal through pornography story ("He Said His Name was Wild Bill" by Marlena Scott on Amazon) published her trauma. She wrote using a pseudonym. I saw her for almost two years and therapy helped to an extent. I recommended that she write down her story, it helped, she started watching her diet, it helped, she did EMDR it helped, she took meds, it helped, but when she chose to go back to her perpetrator, well the rest is history. The problem is the woman was extremely overweight and she didn't do any of the yoga or Mindfulness tools I recommend. I think this lack of addressing the body, led to her irrational choice to go back to her perpetrator when she became too stressed living in the halfway homes she was in. Her amygdala smoke alarm went off after living in a chaotic environment of the halfway home and she bolted for something worse. I'm sorry to say that when she left, she ended up relapsing on meth with the same loser that abused her years ago. She wanted to believe he changed since he told her he would not do those things to her anymore. Yea, right?

PTSD has been shown in positron emission studies (PET scans) to affect the brain. When Rauch, van der Kolk, and colleagues (1996) had patients write a narrative about their trauma they showed heightened activity in the right hemisphere of the brain, areas involved in emotional arousal which may have reflected flash backs. Furthermore, the Broc's area, the left part of the hemisphere responsible for translating personal experiences into communication, turned off. The findings indicated how PTSD changes the neuronal activity in the brain. Van der Kolk with his colleagues went on to study PTSD patients' brain activity with Pre and Post EMDR therapy. He found EMDR therapy may have shown an improvement in the ability to make sense of sensory stimulation. (Rauch, van der Kolk,et al,1996. A symptom provocation study of post traumatic stress disorder using positron emission tomography and script driven imagery. Archives of General Psychiatry, 53, 380-987)

Dana Shepard-Cardwell, M.Ed.

I recently did a weekend workshop with Dr. Bessel van der Kolk and his partner, Licia Sky. The topic was about using nonverbal techniques in therapy. Dr. van der Kolk did one of the first national studies related to yoga and its results helping PTSD Vietnam Veterans. His book *The Body Keeps the Score* shares information on how yoga and other modalities like EMDR, tapping, neurofeedback help reduce the many symptoms related to trauma. Associated symptoms with trauma include: hyperarousal of the limbic brain, avoidance, isolation, anger, numbing out, depression, anxiety, reckless behaviors, GI (gut) issues, somatic issues like headaches and migraines and body pain, dissociation, insomnia, weight gain or weight loss, sexual heightened arousal or lack of libido, sleeping too much, rage, fear, attention problems, lack of organization, erratic thoughts or behaviors, and many more.

Furthermore, Dr. Van der Kolk reported that when something reminds a person of a trauma (unconscious most often related to a sight, sound, smell, or taste) their right brain reacts as if the traumatic event were happening in the present. This is where trauma gets "stuck" in the amygdala (fight, flight, or freeze) and other deep primal parts of the brain and the neurons react so that the synapses don't pass up to the thinking area of the PFC (prefrontal cortex), which is the area of the brain that tells the mind it's just a memory, it's not happening again.

I also did a workshop by Dr. Michelle Riberio titled "Yoga for Trauma" where she noted an estimated 70% of the American citizens will experience a traumatic event at least once during their lifetime and 20% of those who experience trauma will go on to develop symptoms of PTSD. She supported a study that showed when people went through therapy that included yoga there was a 70% satisfaction rate and members showed a decrease in problematic symptoms.

According to Harvard Mental Health studies, yoga can reduce the impact of stress, help decrease anxiety, help decrease symptoms related to depression, and increase one's own soothing techniques to improve overall energy. Yoga used routinely involves using different body poses, while balancing both sides of the body and both sides of the mind. Yoga uses diaphragmatic breathing and meditation. Yoga used in therapy relaxes the body when anxious and helps ease depression by improving concentration, increasing the neurotransmitters serotonin and GABA, and helps balance energy

Dana Shepard-Cardwell, M.Ed.

levels after the session. Yoga therapy has been studied to help people manage mental and emotional problems, decrease low back pain, decrease chronic pain all over the body, improve overall health, and ground a person for better well-being with the ability to handle future problems effectively.

How does violence affect children?

Children exposed to violence are subjected to the risks for neglect, abuse, exposure to trauma, and the loss of one or both of their parents. These traumas can lead to negative outcomes for children and may affect their well-being, safety, and stability. Childhood problems associated with exposure to domestic violence fall into 3 primary categories[3]:

1. Psychological: fear, anxiety, low self-esteem, withdrawal, depression, problematic relationships, higher levels of aggression, anger, hostility, oppositional behavior, and disobedience.
2. Cognitive: lower cognitive functioning, poor school performance, lack of conflict-resolution skills, limited problem-solving skills, pro-violence attitudes, belief in rigid gender stereotypes and male dominance.
3. Long-term: higher levels of depression and trauma symptoms, increased tolerance for and use of violence in adult relationships. (As reported by the OVC, Office for Victims of Crime)

Does childhood violence lead to social deviance? So how do children go from adolescence to an adult perpetrator?
"Is it related to trauma?" Another question is, "Why are some adults sexually attracted to children or adolescents?"

Salter notes it's because they have what is known as "deviant arousal pattern". Furthermore, "it is a particularly vexing group because, for one thing, we don't have a clue how and why a sexual attraction to children develops." The doctor notes that even though we don't know the origins of how child sexual attraction starts, we do know about the patterns it produces, which centers on manipulation often through bribes, gifts, and psychological games.

Think about the Olympic gymnastics' doctor, Larry Nassar, who is now a convicted serial child molester. Many of the girls say he was a

Dana Shepard-Cardwell, M.Ed.

nice person. This during a time when the girls were subjected to ritualistic training, that at times, became bludgeoning. Nassar appeared to care about their well-being and always had an ear open to listen and help. Little did the public know what he was doing behind closed doors with these teens.

Dr. Salter points out that not all offenders have been victims themselves, "*it is most likely that most offenders weren't victims*" specifically referring to adults who are attracted to children or adolescents. Some studies report that the limbic area of sexual deviants is smaller than the average. I don't think therapy would change that person's brain size, do you? The sexual perpetrators don't have hijacked minds, they have Wacked Minds!

My Heart

My heart is hurting
It feels like dirt
It might turn to stone on being alone
I miss my family
I feel like I'm bleeding eternally

My Dad is abusive and aggressive
He makes it seem like he is possessive
He'd throw me over a bridge
 like he was Slamming the fridge
He tried to kill my Mom
And stabbed me in the palm
He made me feel so sad
He's the one who should feel bad

Anger

Anger is something bad.

Dana Shepard-Cardwell, M.Ed.

It usually ends up with everyone sad,
They say that anger is sparked by a demon,
Because of something she or he done,
What happened in my life to me
Is something no one wants to see.
Stuff like therapy and meditation,
Will help us go back into relaxation.
The first step of anger is the fuming,
Normally because of somebody assuming,
The words that come out are vile,
Soon you start sweating like you ran a mile,
The second step is the accusing.
Even though something you thought of was amusing.
I know how it feels.
It makes me not want to eat at meals.
The last step is exploding, mostly from overloading.
But there's a way out of it see?
Trust me because it happened to me.
Just trust in you and you'll be something new.
Maybe put some God in your life
And you'll be as sharp as a knife.

Suicide

I feel like I want to do suicide
It makes me want to die
So I should tell a lie
Man, I am so shy
That's what helps me want to do suicide
But I've learned my lesson now
And I'll tell you how
My life is worth something
Which is better than nothing
You can keep on going now
And If you want to know how
You can live your life right
Instead of getting stabbed by a knife

The Day I was Hurt

Dana Shepard-Cardwell, M.Ed.

"The day I was hurt, I thought I was safe, but every day I think I need to feel safe and loved. I think I need to get help. I think I need to have someone that can love and care for me like my Mom and Dad. But the day I messed up I made a real big mistake, I didn't feel like my family was safe so I ran away. But then I had hope when I went to a mental hospital. I thought I was safe. I thought nobody would hurt me, but knowing you're safe is better than thinking you're safe. I got hurt by kids older, bigger, and stronger than me. I was 13, they were 16, 15,14. It was a lot of my time I was there. I was always getting hurt and one night I was raped. I didn't feel safe anymore. I had to keep it in. I didn't feel like I wanted to tell anybody. I felt like they wouldn't believe me, but I was wrong, and then I finally felt like I should finally let it out, because I couldn't hold it in. And I felt really scared, but then I felt like I could let it go and feel free to be honest about my worries."

Violence

It is a type of anger, but this is bigger.
Your clothes get muddy, while your nose gets bloody.
Both sides throwing punches
And screaming when their bone crunches
People are even shooting one another with a gun,
The worst part is they think it's fun.
They mostly resolve from get backs,
And they mostly fall into setbacks.
When people get killed, all of time gets stilled.
With stuff like the great depression,
The world falls into aggression.
And with things like trauma,
It makes you feel like you're in a boiling hot sauna.
I really hate my dad,
Mostly because he did things that were very bad
And when my mom started doing drugs,
They crawled into her body like bugs.
Now look where I am, watched by millions on cam(era).
The number of times I swear,
Is the number of clothes everybody wears,
Now I write this with a sigh, oh no, it's time to go,
Good Bye!

Inspirational poems by teens I've seen in treatment. (A poem session is offered if they choose. Many just rattle these poems off the top of their heads, never having any experience in poetry. They recite, while I write. Their young survivor souls amaze and inspire me.

35

Dana Shepard-Cardwell, M.Ed.

Perseverance and Resilience to overcome stress

Iron Nugget: How do you build your inner strength? How do you not take conversations out of context when someone may just want to talk to you about something to help you? Aren't we all guilty of reacting and taking things out of context?

I did react negatively, just the other night when I had books spread out in another woman's area and she said, "Is this yours?" I reacted sarcastically with, "Yes! Is it in your way?" My response was short and curt, because I thought her first words were high pitched and annoyed with my books left on a table we were sharing. She came back cocky with me and irritated, after I got irritated, but then she spilled her drink on herself. And the next thing I know is we are giggling and then hashing it out about what just happened and how we falsely reacted to each other. Turns out she just had a heavy southern accent and it was just her voice. Becoming defensive and reacting to people affects us all. The funny part is that we both were calm until we misjudged the other and then we both became *bitchy*. Bitchy is as bitchy does.

All of us can overreact, but how do we take back our hijacked minds and how do we build resilience? Resilience is listed as the capability of a strained body to recover or an ability to recover from or adjust to misfortune or change. Why are some of us like Tigger from Winnie the Pooh and we have these bouncy, bouncy, bounce back ways and others don't?

An article in Prevention magazine by Elaine Chin, M.D. and William Howatt, PH. D. (two smart people because of their education) noted that "resilience is a set of coping mechanisms we develop over time, and research in positive psychology has found that this quality is determined in part by how we take care of ourselves, the people we surround ourselves with, and what we do to find meaning and purpose in our lives." This is pertinent information people! My friend who was miserable with teaching also complained of her 25-pound weight gain, yet she does not exercise at all. Stress kills, but when you don't change your stress, you are just as guilty of landing on your own sword.

Dana Shepard-Cardwell, M.Ed.

When we sit around on autopilot and complain about our circumstances, yet do nothing to change it, we are only making matters worse for ourselves and for those around us. Resiliency specifically comes from getting the F^$& off of autopilot! If you're on Fire, you don't just yell and complain. NO!! You, STOP, DROP, and ROLL! Dr. Chin points out that 40% of our overall happiness is thought to come from our own actions, not from what has happened to us or what's in our genes. Being a resilient Warrior Princess has to do with what thoughts I have and actions I do to become resilient when "bad things happen to good people". I had a self-taught manual years ago by finding my own resilience, but here are some suggestions by the smart, educated doctors in Prevention magazine.

Prevention magazine noted, "A resounding 81% of people who said they didn't deal well with daily stress also felt the least healthy overall." To build your inner strength Dr. Chin and Dr. Howatt give you some new habits to develop. I do a 90 day Reboot for my porn addicted clients and for my unhealthy clients, so I suggest making resilience a new habit, stick with it for 3 months. Here are the doctors' recommendations to develop resilience and take back your hijacked mind: Get plenty of sleep, 7-8 hours (this helps your immune system and your mind) and move your body with 30 minutes of exercise daily. They supported my previous comment on how exercise (I used yoga as an example) increases your feel good neurotransmitters of GABA which calms anxiety and "quiets negative thinking", breathe deeply as "research suggests that meditation may shrink the amygdala reducing stress and anxiety to keep you alert and calm", eat enough (of the right food, not fast foods). They also note finding "your tribe" will help you feel connected and less alone, take 10 minutes of self care each day (taking a bath, reading, brushing your hair and body, using a massage chair, sitting with coffee in the morning, etc.), and just saying kind words to yourself and others each day.

Dr. Dawn Sweet did a study with college students and thinking positively about themselves and those they passed as they walked to class past others. The study found that those involved reported feeling more happiness, lower anxiety, and greater empathy than the others in the study who just walked to class normally.

Making stress relief changes will help take back your hijacked mind, but what if you have had significant trauma and your life seems out of

37

control? What if you didn't have a pleasant childhood? How can those events be affecting you? Your mind has been hijacked, it's OK, you're not crazy, there are solutions.

An article by Zoler titled, "Eye Movement Desensitization: Brain imaging shows benefit of PTSD therapy" in Clinical Psychiatry News (1998) speaks for itself on the benefits EMDR does with allowing the brain to get somewhat unstuck and move the traumatic images through the Adaptive Information Processing model.

Meanwhile… Back at the Ranch…
The Ghostly Skeleton in My Closet

Most victims are assaulted by someone they know. (National Center for Victims of Crime)

After "stairway to hell boyfriend," and the pain in my ass, I dated different boys. I was in my junior year of high school and was still partying but still not promiscuous. So, here I was at age 17. This particular senior football player, I happened to be a "little interested in" drove a really nice, fast sports car and had been "scoping" me out at the last few parties I went to. It started at a town hall dance when he grabbed me and had me sit on his lap. He talked a good game, flirted with me and frankly, I enjoyed the attention. Mr. Football was a big man on campus and known as being cocky and arrogant. He earned respect by being loud and he could get violent at times. We girls tend to have our own games. We don't just fall for whoever asks us out. We have criteria to go by, generally speaking. Not that being athletic, arrogant, and driving a nice car is a good criterion to go by, as I learned later.

After a football game one night, he asked a friend and me to go to a party. I was staying at my friend Ally's home (whose mother would pass out after drinking). Each night was different. She could pass out early or late. We opted for later that night and told Richard (aka. Mr. Football) to park just down the road and pick us up at 11 p.m. On this night, I was staying with Ally's sister, the dark-headed rebel. She was up for some mischief that night, as was I. Ally didn't want any part of what we were doing. In retrospect, I don't blame her!

My friend's mother passed out on time, just after the evening news. We stuffed our bed with pillows and clothes under the sheets. The

Dana Shepard-Cardwell, M.Ed.

next project was the challenge of getting the screen off Lila's window. That one was a booger to get off. We spent probably fifteen minutes working on it. A little muscle, giggling, and a lot of "Shh, she's going to wake-up," and task accomplished. The screen finally came off. I doubt that it was in one piece, though. I think we left a hole in it from finally resorting to using a screwdriver to pry it off.

We had already done our pre-party warm-up exercises, consisting of two rum and Cokes, changing clothes at least three times, and spending time on hair and make-up. After using up a bottle of hairspray and assuring each other that we did not look fat in whatever we were wearing, we were on our way. Mind you, Lila and I were both a size three. How could we ever look fat? The sad part is that most young teens feel this way even today. Granted there are a lot more overweight teens. It's the ones that are in shape that seem to obsess over their image and weight. Lack of self-esteem plays more problems in peer pressure than most adults realize.

We found our ride, waiting down the road. The car lights were off, but when they saw us walking down the street there was a blink on and a blink off signal of where they were. It was pitch dark as Richard and his friend took us to the party just a mile up the road. Lila and I were giggling and looking forward to having fun. We did not sneak out every weekend—this was one of the few times. The party was starting to die down, as it was around 11:30 p.m. and most party-goers had to leave due to curfew. The remainder of the kids were stoned, drunk, or both. There may have been one sober one left in the group, but it did not appear that way. This should have been my first "Ah-ha" sign.

My friend and I were handed drinks immediately as we walked in the door. We drank, we laughed, and we mingled. After we had a drink or two, Richard went upstairs where there was a pool table and gaming going on. The house was full of the haze of smoke and loud rock music boomed throughout. I followed Richard upstairs. I was talking to some guys at the pool table upstairs when Richard yelled down the hall, "Hey Dana, come over here!" where he was standing outside a bedroom. The house was large and the upstairs was huge. There were a lot of rooms upstairs. I walked down to where he was. He told me he wanted to talk, since we did not get much time to talk at school. I remember it was hard to hear, so he closed the door.

39

Dana Shepard-Cardwell, M.Ed.

I didn't think anything of it at the time. Another "Ah-ha" sign missed. He sat on a chair, not the bed. He pulled me to his lap and talked about what seemed like normal conversation. After a while he kissed me. I didn't mind and kissed back. The kissing transferred to the bed. No clothes coming off, just making out. The line crossed after fifteen minutes or so, he started to pull my pants down. I told him, "No." He said, "Yes." I said, "No." He said, "Yes." Until, finally, he said he wasn't going to let me leave until my pants came off, and he pulled them off with me consistently trying to resist. Once "the act" started, all I remember is his heavy breathing, pain, and praying for him to finish already, get off me, and leave me the hell alone.

Once it was over, I ran to the bathroom which was in the same room. I saw a lot of blood once I was in the bathroom. I heard him yell, "You didn't tell me you were a virgin!" and he ran out of the bedroom and then out of the house. I still remember thinking, "That's what it would have taken to keep you from raping me?" "NO!" obviously didn't work, even after numerous attempts. Many young victims don't realize they're being raped until the act has started. The music was so loud at that party; I never yelled, and was basically in shock when "the act" started. I never thought I would lose my virginity violently that night when I set out with a girl friend to "have some fun."

I recently heard a woman on T.V. talk about sexual assault. She noted that people mention the fight or flight response, but she disagreed with the explanation of many sexual assault cases as we tend to know our assailant. The lady shared her theory is a "fight, flight, or freeze" situation. How right she is, I didn't use the fight or flight, I just froze! I'm sure many assaulted survivors would say the same thing; it starts happening and then your brain and body just freeze!

With Richard's running through the house, he caused curiosity with the few partiers that were left. Some guys ran into the room to find out what the commotion was all about, as I was exiting the bathroom. The room looked like a crime scene. There was blood all over the bed, all over the carpet—everywhere. I guess with the forceful nature of the rape, I bled a lot more than a virgin normally would. The depression and PTSD that set in that night followed me for years.

The act of the rape was not as depressing as the stigma that occurred afterwards. No one at that party knew I was raped, they assumed I had sex during my period. There were about five guys who came into that

Dana Shepard-Cardwell, M.Ed.

room and one happened to be Jay, the guy that pushed me down the stairs. Jay was the only one that seemed to know what might have happened as we had dated previously. He knew I didn't sleep around, much less on my period!

Jay, the Royal Pain in the Ass, hugged me and told me it was going to be OK, after everyone was making comments behind my back. He talked with me and truly calmed my state of shock. I was in shock and did not talk after the incident. You would think the other boys would have known something was wrong, as I was hyper and talking non-stop. I was embarrassed and stared at the floor. I made eye contact with none of them. No one knew what happened that night, just that there was a bad scene in guest room No. 5.

The following Monday I could not go to school because my stomach felt so vile. This was the start of a stomach ulcer; which could have started due to all the alcohol I had been drinking or just the psychosomatic problems due to my home life and the rape. Psychosomatic problems are usually physical ailments that start due to psychological stressors. It could be a teenager having a bad headache due to the stress of trying to get into college or just day-to-day stresses. Anything can cause psychosomatic issues: a break up with a boyfriend, being bullied, taking tests, preparing for a football game or perhaps, say, an Ironman. Conflict in the home with parents or siblings can lead to psychosomatic problems. Yelling, loud noises throughout the home. You get the picture.

I had to take prescription medication for several years after developing a nervous stomach. My mother did not know of the incident since it was not a topic of discussion in our house. In fact, no topic was up for discussion in our house. We just didn't talk. Oh, superficial stuff was talked about, but never feelings of frustration and despair. Life was supposed to see through rose- colored glasses. No one in the Shepard family had issues.

I was ashamed of sneaking out and blamed myself for a large part of the incident. Was I wrong for sneaking out and drinking? Yes. Was it OK or my fault for getting raped? NO. Not back then and not now. No teen asks to get raped. Unfortunately, my "Ah-Ha" moment didn't come until after it was too late.

What is Sexual Assault? For sexual activity to be alright, it must be

Dana Shepard-Cardwell, M.Ed.

consensual, which means that both parties want it to happen. Sexual assault is when any person forces you to participate in a sexual act when you don't want to. This includes touching or penetrating the vagina, anus or mouth of the victim, touching the penis of the victim, or forcing the victim to touch the attacker's vagina, penis, or anus.

Touching can mean with a hand, finger, mouth, penis, or just about anything else including objects. It doesn't always take physical force to sexually assault a victim. Attackers can use threats or intimidation to make a victim feel afraid or unable to refuse them. It is also sexual assault if the victim is drunk, drugged, unconscious, too young (ages of consent differ from state to state) or mentally disabled.

Some statistics show one in three women or one in four women have been sexually assaulted at one time in their lives. This accounts for 25 to 33 percent of the female population. Some statistics show that one in six men are sexually assaulted. Some say, "Well if there was no penetration by a penis, then there was no rape." This is a myth. While legal definitions of rape vary from state to state, the National Office of Victims of Crime state that rape constitutes penetration with a penis, finger, foreign object or unwanted touching of sexual body parts without penetration.

The rape wasn't the first sexual assault I had encountered in my life. The first time came with the first boy I kissed, I mean really kissed. Not just a peck. I was in the 8th grade and my friend and I used to walk up to the Jr. High I attended to "play tennis." We weren't there to play tennis. Bret lived near the school and would walk over to flirt with us. From there it became a game of "Will Bret see us?" and let's make-out in the walkway. On one "make out day", Bret grabbed my hand and stuck it down his pants as we were kissing.

I immediately grabbed my hand back, yelled at him, and walked home with my hand extended 3 feet away from the rest of my body. A person passing by would have thought I was reaching up to Heaven in praise or telling someone to "Stop, in the name of Love..." My hand was as far away from the rest of my body as it could go and I was walking as fast as I could. I would have run, but that would have meant my disgusting, germ-filled hand would have to come near my body to propel me forward. I couldn't get home fast enough to wash the grossness off my hand! He had crossed the line by grabbing my

Dana Shepard-Cardwell, M.Ed.

hand and forcing me to do something I had no intention of doing. Sexual assault includes making someone touch your penis/vagina when they have not consented.

Back to the rape aftermath, I couldn't stay home two days in a row, so I had to return to high school and face the music. I walked in the back door of the school that morning and immediately heard people talking about me in whispers. One guy didn't even bother whispering. Fernando was always friendly to me and would occasionally ask me, "When are we going to go out?" I'd laugh but not reply. On this morning, I heard him say in front of his buddies, "And I thought you were a nice girl. You're just a tramp!" I think this hurt as much as the crime. Many years later, I can still hear his words and they sting like a bee each time.

Word spread like wildfire. People started calling me, "Split", behind my back. What a horrible thing! I guess word around campus became that I had sex at a party as a virgin. That part was right, but the rape was never asked, mentioned, or brought up while in high school. I lost my closest friends, except for one. I didn't discuss what happened, ever, even with Lila as we walked home the night of the incident. She didn't ask, if I recall. I do public presentations on sexual assault intervention. With the presentations, I show videos, Power Points slides, and do a Myth or Fact question time with the audience. One question goes like this: "Myth or Fact? When a victim knows her assailant she is more likely to report the rape to the police?"

"Myth! The fact is that the victim who knows her assailant is less likely to report due to self-blame, fear that her friends and family will blame her, and the fact that drugs and alcohol are more likely involved.

Another Myth or Fact: Rape is most often perpetrated by a stranger? Myth, a woman is statistically more likely to be raped by someone she knows. (National Office for Victims of Crime.) Per the National Institute on Alcohol Abuse, more than 696,000 students between ages 18-24 are assaulted by another student who has been drinking. Alcohol plays a huge role on sexual assault.

A report came out a few years back that noted 63 percent of high school seniors have had intercourse. Just think what the percentage might be presently. I attended an STD class by the Texas Department

Dana Shepard-Cardwell, M.Ed.

of Health as a juvenile probation officer that noted 1 in 3 teens that has had sex, has or has had an STD. Can you imagine how many teens you know maybe caring an STD? That's just alarming. Herpes, gonorrhea, chlamydia, AIDS, you name it. And even cancer. Associated Press came out with an article several years' back that stated 70 percent of oral cancer can be linked to HPV.

Let me explain the article. A doctor noted 10 years ago his average oral cancer patients were men over 60 who used tobacco and drank heavily. Today, his patients with oral cancer are the opposite. Dr. Nussenbaum, an ear, nose, throat doctor at Washington University, estimated that 70 percent of his oral cancer patients have tumors on the back of their tongues and tonsils caused by the human papillomavirus-16, otherwise known as HPV. Most of the clients are between the ages of 40 to 50. Experts suggest that all the men and women with the HPV form got it from oral sex. Dr. Nussenbaum stated that 98 percent of cervical cancer is caused by HPV, and mainly the HPV-16. No one talks about how you can get mouth cancer. It's taboo or not discussed, yet middle-aged women are walking around with canker sores and suffering tremendous pain from tongue and tonsil tumors.

The article from St. Louis (AP) goes on to note that Dr. Harald zur Hausen, a German doctor and scientist, was awarded the Nobel Prize for medicine for finding the human papilloma viruses that can cause cervical cancer, the second most common cancer among women. The Nobel assembly noted that Dr. zur Hausen went against current dogma in the 1970s when he discovered that certain types of HPV caused the cancer and that the DNA of HPV could be found in tumors.

Think of the 1970s. Ahh... the freedom movement, during and just after Vietnam. World peace, do what feels groovy, "good." Love your neighbor, get a VW van, have lots of love sessions. You get the picture. Peace and love were everywhere. Now those women have grown up and are suffering the consequences. We have studies now to change the future epidemic, though.

The Internet suggests it wasn't until 2000 that John Hopkins Kimmel Cancer Center reported a link between HPV and specific throat cancers. Medical experts suspect the increase in HPV oral cancer stems from a shift in sexual behaviors about 40 years ago. Did I not

Dana Shepard-Cardwell, M.Ed.

just mention the love and peace era? Now, we don't have to be a genius to figure out that there was going to be some sort of issue arising from that much love going on. Immorality? Revelation 21:8 reads, "But the cowardly, the unbelieving, the vile, the murderers, the sexually immoral, those who practice magic, the idolaters, and all liars—their place will be in the fiery lake of burning sulfur." I'll leave the interpretation to you.

Cancer from the HPV virus often develops on the tonsils notes one website. Should we suggest that all teens have a tonsillectomy? How about telling them that numerous sexual partners and oral sex partners is not the answer to live a long and productive life? How about actually talking about it and not just teaching abstinence in the schools? Seriously? Telling a kid, "Don't do it!" doesn't work.

I know that when I was younger if my mother said to wear the pretty blue outfit; I was picking the red one, just because. Simply telling a kid, "No" is not the answer. They are probably more likely to go in the opposite direction. Teens need to develop their own identity and fight their own battles, but with your love and support. We don't send our soldiers to war and then say, "See you when you kill all the enemies and come back home!" Talk to teens, discuss, explain, and let them make their decision because they are ultimately the one in control of their decisions and their bodies. They need to hear from you over and over, not like a broken record, but in a sing-song kind of way. Encourage them to join in on the song. It can be a duet!

The John Hopkins study compared healthy people to those with the HPV oral cancer and concluded that people with the HPV virus were 32 percent more likely to develop oral cancer than those without. People who had more than six oral sex partners were 8.6 times more likely to develop HPV linked cancer. So, now society comes out with Gardasil, a drug that helps protect against human papillomavirus. Is this the answer? What are the ramifications from this drug down the road? I remember when birth control first came out. Studies now show there were serious detrimental factors with the birth control of our mothers and grandmothers.

Is the solution to go get this injection and have all the sex you want? Hmmm... doesn't seem like the best answer. The choice is ultimately yours. Do you want to be promiscuous and take a shot for preventative reasons not knowing the long-term side-effects or live

Dana Shepard-Cardwell, M.Ed.

your life in a manner that warrants pride and increased self-esteem in the long run? Experts suggest that the HPV lies dormant for years, perhaps decades, before causing cancer. Should middle-aged women in their 40s and younger consider getting vaccinated with the Gardasil, also? Better yet, older women who were sexually active years ago?

Should we suggest that most of the population get vaccinated from HPV? No expert knows how long the disease can sit dormant because there has been so little data on the disease. A fact that cannot be disputed is that the National Cancer Institute recently determined that the rate of oral cancer caused by HPV has risen significantly since 1973.

Laura Beil, notes that when children shroud their behavior in secrecy, they lose open, caring connections to adults who can help them make thoughtful decisions. These connections are especially important in matters of sex. Particularly since the stakes are high and sex seems ubiquitous in the popular culture. She notes that today that almost eight-in-ten prime time shows contain sexual content, with an average of nearly six sex-related scenes per hour. You don't think your child is impressed by this? You can sure bet they are.

A few years back the fad was "The Choking Game" and kids were dying left and right from what they thought was a fun "natural high". Now, we have the world wide web to thank for "fapping" and kids thinking kinky sex is a normal. Fapping was coined from Chinese illegal websites for pornography as it correlated to masturbating to porn. Unfortunately, the hipsters are in the world of money making and constantly looking for new fads to persuade children and teens to become "click happy", further corrupting society and our children.

The drive for profits and the extreme affects all of us! And those hipsters find ways to lure children and teens into their unfiltered internet pornography. Kids become interested, confused, and ultimately lost. They develop hijacked minds and become addicted to the web. It creeps up on the adolescents and they start thinking this is normal. It becomes what they "think" is a natural high, but it's an addicting high that demands more and more extreme behaviors. Research supports the idea that the fap addict turns luring other teens into their extreme world with peer pressure and bullying and the prey becomes the predator. Studies have also found that fappers have

46

Dana Shepard-Cardwell, M.Ed.

shorter attention spans and lack energy to complete simple and basic tasks. They are zombie-fied with hijacked minds and it alters their brain chemistry.

"Sadomasochism, welfare, crystal meth, cocaine, a life of crime, and even prison await the young man who has tumbled into this downward spiral" (www.harddawn.com, Bacon,2013,"Fapping the newest internet fad that could be putting your teens at risk"). Thank goodness there are "No-fap" support groups and websites to help break the addiction of pornography.

Parents often underestimate their own importance and ignore the difficult topics. Brown's anti-teen- pregnancy campaign has found that kids, when asked about the most influential voices in their decisions to have sex, rate their parents influence higher than their peers or the media. Even when you preach, parents. They know you love them and you care. Discussion rather than preaching is always more productive. No one likes a boss who comes in and tells you how to do every minute of your job. You can think for yourself and therefore take care of business, just with a little direction and intervention. Use open ended questions to help your child or teen. Ask if they know of someone who spends too much time on the internet and if they have seen changes in that person. Bring up stats on FB addiction, SnapChat addiction, Tweeting, Instagram, pornography addiction.

Studies show 80 to 90 percent of teens talking with parents, openly, helps delay sex. My husband and I have been bantering for years. My husband is a psychologist, and from the beginning of our relationship knew about my experience. I told him that when we had kids I would scare the crap out of them from drinking, smoking, or having sex due to my experiences. It would be such an unpleasant talk that they wouldn't even want to go there.

Smashing happens! (Teen slang for sex.) A famous sex therapist noted that talking to kids in kindergarten is when the sex topic shoud happen, before it becomes funny and words like my "who ha", "cookie", "vajayjay", "nippy", "ding dong", "ding a ling", "peepee", "elephant trunk" "weiner".

He calmly told me that scaring our kids would not be the answer and of course, he was right. We only had one child, a beautiful girl, at that. When our little girl was 9 years old, I hadn't had the birds and bees talk, yet, but don't think the Kardashins and all the tween shows didn't expose her. She was at a friend's house one week when she came home and asked, "Mom, what does it mean when it breaks?" Hm... Now she knows what happens if you break jewelry, eggs in a pan, dishes, etc. This must be more serious or sensitive. "Where was this going?" I was washing dishes and so not prepared for this talk. Think calmly. Think about what your husband has been telling you all these years.

"Breaks?" I asked her. "What breaks?" She goes on to say, "Well, Meg and I were watching Sisterhood of the Traveling Pants II, and this guy came out of the bathroom, saying it broke. Meg told me that it was something that kept a girl from getting pregnant."
Think...Don't preach...Think. Don't preach. "Well", I said," First of all, what rating was this show? Sounds like PG-13, and you are not 13. It says PG-13 for a reason." OK, I started off preaching, but I held back.

She said she didn't know what rating it was, but that they had checked it out and it wasn't bad. I told her, "It sounds like they were doing things that teens should not do at their age. Something that you should wait to do until you're married." Preaching... preaching. I then addressed the question. "What they were referring to was probably a condom. Something a man puts on his "weeny," (yes, I used the word 'weeny') as a form of protection from disease and getting a girl pregnant."

Did I mention Meg has two older sisters? Don't think older siblings aren't exposing our kids to sex when they overhear older phone conversations and computer dialogue. I admit, I did not handle that situation anything like I would have hoped. Teens talk with someone, don't wait until you are leaving that party after being raped or pressured into something you haven't prepared yourself for. Parents talk to your kids. (This part came from my book, Hyper, and was written when my daughter was younger and we were just learning how to parent a pre-teen. She turned out pretty good so far, as a collegiate cheerleader, psych major, and a UCA instructor.)

Beverly Engel writes in her book, The Right to Innocence. Healing the Trauma of Childhood Sexual Abuse, "What are the specific benefits of recovery?" She lists these headlines related to the benefits:

Dana Shepard-Cardwell, M.Ed.

"higher self-esteem, improved relationships, improved sexuality, increased ability to express emotions, relief from physical symptoms, greater sense of control, heightened self-awareness, staying grounded in the present, developing healthier defenses, and greater peace of mind." I recommend this book to those who endured childhood sexual trauma, whatever it was. This book could save your soul!

Most importantly, remember; don't try to analyze a personality disorder (anti-social). Just leave. It won't help and doesn't work trying to figure them out. You never will. Run Away. (Call the cops, first!)

Love your neighbor as yourself as long as they aren't a criminal personality. I talk with teens about the two laws in life, Man's law and God's law. Doing and thinking negatively got me nowhere as a teen and young adult. I felt like Pig Pen from Charlie Brown with dust and dirtiness following me at all times. The more negative I was, the more negative my life became. I did get my prayers answered for my dream man. But eating bad, thinking pessimistically, anger, chaos, etc had all consumed my mind, body, and soul.

I knew I needed a change and didn't know where to turn. My future husband was my ROCK, but I didn't want to let him know how hard it was for me to hold my Shit together each day or he may cut and run.

Check out these videos on **You Tube**:

"I Am a Victim of Sexual Assault. MyLifeAsEva"

"E60: The RA Dickey Story" (male sexual assault)

"My Story/Elizabeth Smart"

"Through Our Eyes: Children, Violence, and Trauma"

"How Childhood Trauma Affects Health Across a Lifetime" Nadine Burke Harris

"Bessel van der Kolk: Overcome Trauma with Yoga"

Websites for assistance: The National Center for Victims of Crime, www.ncvc.org   Sex Etc.- Sex Ed by Teens, for Teens, www.sexetc.org   Sexual Abuse Statistics, www.prevent-abuse-now.com

Dana Shepard-Cardwell, M.Ed.

Drugs and Alcohol

In his book, *Inside the Criminal Mind*, Dr. Stanton Samenow, reports that "the public is in danger of being fooled into thinking that marijuana is relatively harmless." He alarms the reader that the adolescent who starts with long term marijuana use generally develops a psychological damage called "a motivational syndrome" as the frequent user turns off and drops out of normal life by rejecting his family, school, and responsible peers. Furthermore, the doctor notes that once the chronic marijuana user starts associating with other drug users after rejecting "normal" peers, he is exposed to other drugs. This is where the crossover to other drugs starts. The user develops a tolerance and an addiction to drugs in general may develop and become "his entire way of life".

The brain is altered with chronic drug use, plain and simple. The facts have been shown over and over with technology showing images of the brain. Drug use "causes changes in the brain and nervous system" (Samenow, 2004). The brain and CNS damage lead to deregulated mood disruptions and criminal activities that a person may not resort to while not using drugs or alcohol. Drugs and heavy alcohol use skew normal judgement.

Dr. Samenow shares, "Criminals exercise the greatest precautions to avoid being caught." Dating back to Freud's time, a clinician can extrapolate that some criminals feel relief when getting caught as it is a subconscious cry for help. These are the people who can objectively receive help, unlike the psychopath/antisocial personality who lacks the moral compass to change or even recognize what he is doing is wrong.

When working with delinquents I agree with Dr. Glasser's assessment that, "delinquents in institutions may resist therapy. The proper function of any treatment institution is to provide a warm, disciplined atmosphere in which the inmates are required to assess their behaviors in terms of responsibility. Institutions which do not do so are only prison. The inmates learn nothing except to deny reality further."

The treatment center where I see boys doesn't refer to them as inmates, they aren't in jail, but I do agree with Dr. Glasser's

Dana Shepard-Cardwell, M.Ed.

approach. I have seen thugs, drug addicts, sexual perpetrators, assailants, and so forth arrive at the treatment center leave a different and better person because of the treatment approach that helps these young boys accept responsibility for their behaviors.

Dr. Glasser shares his take on happiness, "Happiness occurs most often when we are willing to take responsibility for our behavior. Irresponsible people, always seeking to gain happiness without assuming responsibility, find only brief periods of joy, but not the deep seated satisfaction which accompanies responsible behavior." For example, "when they have a problem they may try to ignore it, drown it in drugs or alcohol, or rationalize it away, all in an effort to gain brief happiness." Think about it, what person who sweeps their problems under the rug lives a happy life?

I was supposed to help a troubled young man with EMDR. This young man had a story of not being helped after his trauma of being sexually assaulted as a teen, self medicating, failing to take the medication he was prescribed because he felt it wasn't working, and as a result of his trauma 14 lives have been lost due to what started as one perp's mission to molest young boys. I truly believe the 14 lives lost in that vehicular homicide incident would still be here if that 19 year old got help at age 12/13, when he was first being molested by a teacher.

Some studies show 1 in 6 males under 24 has been sexually assaulted. Without proper intervention, these boys will turn into criminals, because the brain remains on fire from hypervigilance and the inability to relax or calm down. The amygdala stays stuck in fight or flight. These teens with hijacked minds look like criminals, often, but it's just their way of dealing with the hijack. They act out, they can't sit still, they're angry, they become impulsive, they are unorganized, and have a hard time focusing, so then we over-medicate them by taking them to the doctor/s or they get illegal drugs from their peers and self-medicate themselves. It makes sense that they break the law sooner or later when their undeveloped minds aren't equipped to deal with the trauma. They are just looking for something to make themselves feel better.

Come to find out my recent perpetrator was doing just that, trying to find happiness through drugs, alcohol, and internet porn addiction. His short term life of happiness landed him in prison.

Dana Shepard-Cardwell, M.Ed.

"Are we crazy?
Living our lives through a lens
Trapped in our white picket fence
Like ornaments
So comfortable, we're living in a bubble, bubble
So comfortable, we cannot see the trouble, trouble"
(Chained to the rhythm, Katy Perry)

Don't mistake that criminals start out as wayward adolescents. Many
of them victimize not only others around them, but also their own
siblings and parents. Parents generally want the best for their kids. As
Dr. Samenow points out, "There comes a time when parents of such a
child have to face the fact that they are powerless to change the
course of events." It's the teen's choice to continue problematic
behaviors and he/she should not be allowed to destroy the rest of the
family for their decision to be a criminal. In the drug and alcohol
world we talk to families about healthy detachment. You can still love
your family member who has an addiction, but you can't continue to
allow them to steal, lie, and manipulate the family. Kick them out, get
them help, and close the door until they can prove consistency in a
change.

What makes a criminal? Recognize that psychologists note one's
temperament is born with him or her. "From the cradle, the infant's
temperament has a considerable impact on how his parents treat him"
(Samenow, 2004). "No one knows why the criminal opposes the
social order from an early age. No one has yet been successful in
identifying the critical factors that cause criminality. Efforts to help
criminals change have been met with even less success" (Samenow,
2004).

Dr. Samenow reminds us that the psychopath is "characterized as
lacking a sense of responsibility, the capacity to profit from
experience, and a conscience. He is described as impulsive,
emotionally immature, grandiose, and self-centered, and unable to
experience guilt or form meaningful human relationships." The
doctor points out that clinicians may call the psychopath impulsive;
however, "he has a rational, calculating mind that enables him to
delay gratification if he deems it in his best interest."

Dana Shepard-Cardwell, M.Ed.

"Inside the Criminal Mind" points out that a barrier to understanding the criminal or psychopath (antisocial personality) is that most clinicians use interviewing techniques that "are appropriate for many types of clients or patients, but are counterproductive when utilized with a criminal population" (Samenow, 2004). "Said one offender about his doctor, 'She had her theory. I fed her what she wanted to hear until she thought I was cured.'"

My goal as a therapist is to rehabilitate the deviant or addict who has been hurt and tends to hurt others (hurt people hurt people) but I don't get involved with psychopaths. Trying to rehab psychopaths will leave the old adage of "the counselor who works harder than the client" and that job becomes too frustrating. I also love to work with victims, regardless of their gender, sexuality, race, past, future, passivity, aggression, etc. Helping victims become survivors is a very rewarding process.

For the offender who needs to change and has a capacity to do so, we look at recidivism. "Recidivism is the major measure to change." "Of 300,000 prisoners released in 1994 in 15 states, 67.5% were rearrested within a few years." The stats are not promising. This basically implies that only 30% of those released from prison are not true anti-socials, that they can and will change, but the others, almost 70% lack the ability to change and will continue to victimize others. I have read promising changes related to prison systems that use yoga and therapy to decrease recidivism and increase self compassion and compassion toward others. Let's make it a grassroots effort to include yoga and therapy in all prison systems.

Dana Shepard-Cardwell, M.Ed.

Stalking the Stalker

My first time at the Penitentiary included a two hour talk with my stalker, a meek middle aged man with "coke bottle" glasses and a receding hairline, through the hand held phone behind a dirty glass window. Chris noted his childhood was normal besides the fact that he was "bullied all the time" up until 8th grade. It got a little better, but he hated going to school in High School and noted he barely graduated his senior year. He talked about hanging with the wrong crowd in high school and getting into drinking alcohol and smoking weed. Chris talked about making bad choices and breaking into cars to get alcohol and drug money. He shared that he got caught and the court system made him a deal that if he joined the military, he would not have to serve time.

The perp, Chris, talked about some minor disciplinary actions in the military and then having to see the doctor for a psychological evaluation which he noted, "I guess they saw something on it because they honorably discharged me at a year and a half." He shared that the military never told him what they found on his evaluation. He noted different jobs and getting associated back with his old crowd who did a lot of drinking, marijuana, and they introduced him to the world of cocaine.

Chris talked about his family life being stable as his mother taught pre-kindergarten and his step-father worked as well. He noted his biological father was not in his life as the case is with many young people in jail. He noted an advantage of knowing his father unlike many in prison. Chris denied being in Special Education or being on prescription medication at a young age, but did note his mother noticed he looked depressed and took him to the doctor where he was able to get on antidepressant medication. Chris talked about going to a psychiatrist in his late 20s who diagnosed him as bipolar and put him on mood stabilizers which he noted seemed to help. He admitted using uppers, cocaine, and then downers of weed and/or alcohol to feel part of society. He shared how he often felt or feels like an outcast and socially awkward.

My stalker acknowledged being a loner and not fitting in most of his life and his first sexual experience being at 20 with a prostitute. He shared having only one girlfriend for about a month, "But then she moved away". He reported first noticing an interest in the female body when he was about 5 with another little girl and showing their body parts, "I just remember her pink area". He remembered a time

Dana Shepard-Cardwell, M.Ed.

at age 7 when some boys older than him started fondling the babysitter who let them and watching and just "remembering the smell of hairspray and sweat." Chris shared that he gets stuck on smells and colors and noted that he blanked out after the boys started doing things with the babysitter. He shared a time of being confused and obsessed with female clothes.

Chris's obsession with porn started at puberty when he would find Hustler magazines in the woods near his home. He admitted he started putting the bodies of the porn stars on the heads of popular girls at school "that I could never have a chance with" in his school annuals. "Inability to control porn use and/or use that interferes with one's life are two signs of porn addiction." (www.yourbrainonporn.com)

The website also noted that a porn addict's "priorities have shifted due to changes in the brain." So true, the top notch female detective who worked the case noted that Chris was on the porn websites all hours of the day. She noted, "This guy is sick."

"A 2015 study on sex clinic patients found 71% of men who masturbated to porn more than 7 hours a week reported sexual dysfunctions. 33% of those had ejaculation problems. Others reports on porn use correlated regular porn use with lower sexual desires or difficulty climaxing with partners." (www.yourbrainonporn.com) The Science of Pornography Addiction on You Tube noted 25% of the internet searches are porn related! Drugs and pornography are addictive and lead to an increase in tolerance, lead to compulsive behaviors, and have a loss of control. Both have withdrawal symptoms.

Addictions rewire the developing brain. One must realize that an addictive personality is *Not* a prerequisite of getting hooked on porn. Many of the porn addicted guys had no addiction in their family and had no previous addictions. The porn industry is a super stimulus and is said to make more money than Major League Baseball. It is secretive though, ranges show from 6 billion a year revenue to 100 billion a year. On an interesting side note, the global market for psychotropic medications was worth 88 billion in 2015. Do you think these markets care about your welfare?

Chris recognized that he had no real relationships with women in his life. Recently, he became a born again Christian while off drugs and alcohol and being locked-up in prison. He spent a month in solitary confinement after "a nervous breakdown" in one of the temporary

55

placements, but found reading the Bible daily helped him through his rough spell. Chris shared that he read the Daily Bread devotional each day, along with his Bible and The Purpose Driven Life. He talked about his cousin having a mission outreach in SA and it helped him to answer assignments she sent him. He talked about porn being the devil's work and the sin of the flesh getting in his mind where he became consumed with it.

Chris noted his psychiatrist didn't even talk about his porn addiction which led Chris to believe that psychiatrists "are just there as a business to take people's money." He noted his psychiatrist diagnosed him bipolar quickly without any formal assessments. Chris pondered out loud that he wondered if doctors really know what is going on with their patients. (I must say I agree.) Chris reported that he shared things with me that he said he never told his psychiatrist. When I asked why he didn't share those things with his psychiatrist, he said it was because they were never brought up or his doc never asked. I asked a lot of questions because I wanted to know what makes a sexual deviant, a person who cyber stalks people, and who allows porn to become something so out of hand to making it into fantasy relationships. To thinking we were his pieces of Ass?

I came home from that visit and immediately went for a jog to process the intense meeting.

I noticed jogging after the visit and hearing the song "Therapy Session" and "You Love Me Anyway". "The question was raised as my conscience fell a silly little lie. It didn't mean much but it lingers still in the corners of my mind, still you call me to walk on the edge of this world to spread my dreams and fly. But the future's so far, my heart is so frail, I think I'd stay inside. But you love me anyway it's like the nothing in life That I've never known Yes You love me anyway, Oh Lord how YOU love me." (song by, Sidewalk Prophets)

So, what changed for Chris? Was it being away from substances for 11 months and being able to think clearer and how God is more important today in his life to "just take each day as it comes". He noted many of the men are very young in prison and he is glad he wasn't one of the young people because there is a process to go through, but being "an old man in here, they don't mess with you as much". He talked about coming out of his shell some at the Dominguez prison unit, "You have to get to know each personality and nuances or quirks of each in a cell pod." He recognized trying to help the younger men when they wanted to listen, but most often they

56

Dana Shepard-Cardwell, M.Ed.

are set in their ways and don't associate with him. He noted his bunkmate was a heroin addict and how hard life had been for his bunkmate. Chris shared being glad he had a home and was not out on the street like many. He noted most of the guys in the pen he would have never associated with in the real world.

Chris admitted not being able to think clearly or straight when he was evaluated and admitted the last 20 years being a "blur". He admitted crimes (like stealing from employers for his drug habit) and disturbances "all done under the influence" and how he may not have done those things if he had been clean.

Chris noted he often wonders what will happen with his life after he gets out since he has a record now. It appeared as though he wanted to find self worth through his ability to work or get a job. When meeting with him I wondered if he recognized his struggles might be related to trying to create a personification he wanted to be, but wasn't. By that I mean his wanting to be a lady's man and his porn addiction. It's interesting how he would need uppers and downers to feel something in his life instead of feeling alone and depressed, which was the case.

From Dr. Amen's clinic **The Power of Ostracism…..**
It's often been noted that rejection is among the most painful of human emotions. Anyone who has felt the sting of rejection, ostracism or shunning knows how deeply these experiences sting.

According to a Purdue University expert, ostracism can cause pain that often is deeper and lasts longer than a physical injury.

"Being excluded or ostracized is an invisible form of bullying that doesn't leave bruises, and therefore we often underestimate its impact," said Kipling D. Williams, a professor of psychological sciences. "Being excluded by high school friends, office colleagues, or even spouses or family members can be excruciating." "When a person is ostracized, the brain's dorsal anterior cingulate cortex, which registers physical pain, also feels this social injury," Williams said.

Fundamental and foundational for our human needs are the feelings of belonging. Exclusion or ostracism is so painful because it threatens these needs and the core of our self-esteem. "Again and again research has found that strong, harmful reactions are possible even when ostracized by a stranger or for a short amount of time," said Williams.

Dana Shepard-Cardwell, M.Ed.

More than 5,000 people have participated in studies using a computer game designed by Williams to show how just two or three minutes of ostracism can produce lingering negative feelings. Even when being ignored briefly by strangers, with whom the individual will never have any face-to-face interaction, the negative effect is powerful and consistent. This was true even with a great variety of personalities.

After my meetings with Chris I had a conversation with my friend Gina about being stalked and learning from the "stalker" in jail. General topics and then just accidently saying his name. She stopped and said, "Oh my! I know him. I went to elementary school with him." She talked about how she remembered he was always in trouble and how she felt sorry for him. Gina noted she felt he brought a lot of his struggles on himself by instigating others and she even remembered he would "do things like lift girls' dresses up and get in trouble for doing that". She remembered him doing things against the social norm at a young age and not learning from getting in trouble or being out-casted and not appearing to want to fit in. As if he just didn't give a damn, and did as he pleased.

Reality therapy is a true test to see if people are willing to change their bad habits. Questions I use from Reality Therapy include, "What one thing will you do today to start changing your life? To get along better with others? To get what you want in an appropriate manner?" A client must be willing to start today, not another day, if they are truly motivated.

"Well begun is half done" (Aristotle).

Dana Shepard-Cardwell, M.Ed.

Secrets and Violence

Violence destroys neural pathways of children. See www.changingmindsnow.org. The developing brain is not equipped to handle the stress of violence. Exposure to violence leads to impulsive behaviors, drug and alcohol issues, delinquency, anger, depression, fear, and anxiety in children and teens. The good news is that the damage can be reversed by comforting those exposed, showing compassion, lending an ear through reflective listening, giving them new ideas as positive coping tools, complimenting their strengths, and not walking away from them when they are acting out.

Thousands of studies over the past 40 years support the idea that media violence does cause harm to children and led them to become aggressive. In the YouTube video "Desensitized: Media Violence and Children", you can see the facts related to this correlation. The video reports that most kids spend 4 hours a day in front of a screen, and this is even on school days. These kids were 60% more likely to be involved in assaults and fights. Scary TV was associated with internalized emotions of fear, anxiety, and depression. Children become desensitized to violence. Furthermore, aggressive video games increase that desensitization with more and more violent games that raise the reward system.

I recently contacted a young client in prison to get his story in the hope of helping him get his story of being re-victimized out to the masses. Here is his reply, "Dear Dana, I hope this letter finds you well. Thank you for your letter, I hope all is well. Please, tell Eric I said Hello and Thank you very much for all the help he gave me after the accident. I will put you on the visitors list, but it might take some time as nothing happens quick down here. If you're wondering, I'm doing OK down here. I stay to myself and avoid the trouble. I believe it may take 4-5 months to change my list but I will let you know as soon as you are on it. As for the books, thank you very much, but I don't want you to spend any money on me. Thank you M'am. Anyways, thank you very much for your card and I look forward to hearing back from you. Till next time, have a blessed day. Sincerely, Jack."

Dana Shepard-Cardwell, M.Ed.

This poor young man just needed to get his own hijacked brain back to normal after his first trauma as a teen. He never did and the outcome of that tragic event resulted in 14 lives lost, along with the grief associated with all involved. Tragic for those who died and for Jack and his family who lost a young man, as well.

Have you ever noticed the Caution Label on psych meds? Have you thought about how many times one med tends to lead to higher doses eventually, or more medication or many other changes in meds? If you're taking antidepressants are you on that same drug at the same dose 5 years later? Have you changed medications? Have you added benzos for anxiety, pain pills, ADHD meds, mood stabilizers? How many of you are on the same psychotropic medication that you started with? And how many of you are on just one medication? As I mentioned earlier, the psychotropic pharmaceutical companies made over 88 billion in 2015. It's a money making business, just like the porn industry is a billion dollar money making business. Both businesses, psychotropic meds and porn, will do whatever it takes to sell their product, the almighty dollar is what drives them, not your sanity. By the way, it costs nothing to exercise and do yoga to help decrease depression and anxiety. OK, maybe a yoga mat, but that's cheap!

Have you ever read the warning label on Adderall that when it's combined with a serotonin reuptake antidepressant, it can lead to serotonin overload? Serotonin syndrome can cause shivering, diarrhea, muscle rigidity, fever, seizures and can be fatal if not treated as noted by the Mayo Clinic. I had my own reaction to Prozac years ago when the doctor increased my dose when the original prescription dosing didn't help. I became almost comatose one night, my muscles locked-up, I couldn't move or talk for a period of a few hours, it was the scariest experience ever. When I let the doc know, he did what most do, changed my anti-depressant. I was only in my 20s and I thought back then, "doctors know best". NOT!

I just spoke with two different ladies a week ago who recently had similar reactions to antidepressants of seizures, muscles being rigid and lack of focus or control over the mind and body. One lady was a client and noted she had to cancel her session because it took her two days to be able to get out of bed due to the adverse reactions. She had just started trying an antidepressant and the other lady had recently taken an antidepressant for 2-3 weeks. They didn't notice any change,

60

so their respective doctors increased the medication which led to their intense reactions listed above. It scared them immensely. Rightfully so!

The Mayo Clinic notes serotonin overload symptoms include:
Agitation or restlessness
Confusion
Rapid heart rate and/or high blood pressure
Dilated pupils
Loss of muscle control or twitching
Muscle rigidity
Sweating
Diarrhea
Headache
Shivering and unconsciousness

On SECRETS

I tell teens that keeping secrets will slowly kill us. When you tell the truth of shame, guilt, resentment, anger, fear, depression, anxiety, etc, then your life is transformed. Free your soul from the slavery of secrets. How does one answer the life giving question, "Who Am I?" with secrets? Don't let the chains of secrets affect who you could be or who you want to be. The truth needs to be set free. The truth WILL set you free.

Just let the secrets go, be set free from shame, guilt, anger, resentment, and fear. It takes a Warrior with courage to talk about their secrets; a fool allows himself to be chained to the secrets and stay resistant to change. Change comes from speaking up and speaking out with someone you trust.

A therapist friend of mine who uses the "What if" scenario, shared, What is it you want? And if you had that, how would things be? And if things were like that, how would you feel/be? And if you were that way, how would you feel? Think of that one word. Is it happy, free, having fun, peaceful, calm, not afraid? What is holding you back? Perhaps, you might start with sharing your secrets with a therapist.

Dana Shepard-Cardwell, M.Ed.

I saw a bright young man who was in recovery. Nice looking 20 something young man, athletic, arrogant, cocky, but open to change. His secret was that he traded one addiction for another. Drugs for porn. He also noted having a questionable sexual assault type incident as a young teen, which left him wondering about homosexuality, which he denied. Many young males will have a same sex incident as a teen, but not necessarily be homosexual, it's just an experimental stage. Some males move on after a same sex incidence, others become almost traumatized. In this young man's case, as with many, his friend did a truth or dare and the dare won. The result was each guy would perform oral sex on the other. This led to years of confusion for him.

His porn addiction started with the computer then led to picking up girls wherever he could find them, then to the immediate gratification of using prostitutes. He was embarrassed since he was a tall, good looking young man and basically didn't need all-girls, but when his hand didn't do the job and he couldn't find a quickie from girls he had met, he resorted to call-girls.

He was even robbed and beaten by one prostitute and he knew the dangers. His progress was improving; however, he would never use the steps we discussed in therapy like yoga classes, exercising at the gym, support groups, healthy eating, no porn, etc and he eventually relapsed on his drug of choice and lost his job. Friends, we have to break the chains that bind us with new and healthy habits to move to the "What if" answer. Nothing worth having comes easy.

One statistic from Metro Health in San Antonio noted that 1 in 3 teens or young adults having sex has had or currently has an STD. And that doesn't stand for Seriously Tall Date, that stands for Sexually Transmitted Disease. One of my teen clients put it so eloquently, "No matter what you do to hide it, the truth always has a way of rising to the surface." Wow. That boy should get a Nobel Peace Prize. The secrets we try to hide, fester like a boil, and boils sooner or later come to a head and rise to the surface pressing and prodding to be released one way or another. Usually it hurts so bad, we need to seek help to release the tension. Therapy can help release the pain and burden of our secrets we try to ignore or hide. Even if one isn't burdened by trauma, therapy can still help with daily stress and pain that lies dormant in our minds and body.

Dana Shepard-Cardwell, M.Ed.

GOT PIED? P.I.E.D.

P.I.E.D. Porn Induced Erectile Dysfunction
"Porn induced erectile dysfunction is a new controversial theory for explaining sexual problems." (www.medicalnewstoday.com)

A current argument is that porn can desensitize sexual response. "A 2016 article argues that more young men are seeking help for ED, erectile dysfunction, and this could be due to the desensitizing effect of hardcore pornography." The article goes on to say that "the use of pornography may change the way the brain reacts to arousal, making a man less likely to feel aroused by a real-life partner." (www.medicalnewstoday.com)

Think about it, sex with a partner is more physical and less visual. Pornography is visual first, with the man or woman masturbating, leading to the physical release. A visual stimulation gets the physical areas stimulated, but in physical sexual intercourse the visual is not there. Unless of course a person needs to watch porn while they are having intercourse with their partner, which has been the case with some of those addicted to porn.

 A review with clinical reports published 8/16 asked "Is internet pornography causing sexual dysfunction?" (Brian, Wilson,et.al). One abstract shared, "Traditional factors that once explained men's sexual difficulties appear insufficient to account for the sharp rise in erectile dysfunction, delayed ejaculation, decreased sexual satisfaction, and diminished libido during partnered sex in men under 40." That study went on to note, "Alterations in the brain's motivational system are explored as a possible etiology underlying pornography related sexual dysfunction." The review considered "Evidence that internet pornography's unique properties may be potent enough to condition sexual arousal to aspects of internet pornography used that do not readily transition to real life partners, such that sex with desired partners may not register as meeting expectations and arousal declines."

The study in 2012 found that in the past men under 40 did not generally have sexual disturbances (less than 2%), as testosterone levels don't generally start decreasing until middle age. The report noted that the first internet "porn tube sites" appeared around 2006. The report found that in the last decade there has been an increase in

63

Dana Shepard-Cardwell, M.Ed.

sexual difficulties among young men. This problem is not only in the US, as one may equate the rise in problems to obesity; however, the problem has been shown in Swiss men, Italian men, and French men who generally don't have a high obesity rate such as in the US.

Erectile dysfunction was the most common disturbance found (26%) followed by low sexual desire (24%) to problems with orgasm (11%). Another study by the same group in 2016 assessed sexual problems in adolescents aged 16-21 for two years. The results in at least one wave for males found persistent problems were low sexual satisfaction (47.9%), low desire (46%), and even problems with erectile function (45.3%).

Porn addiction can be a hard thing to treat, as many men don't admit to their problems with the pornography and moderation can be hard. It, porn, becomes a "dangerous outlet because changes in the brain go unseen by the person and the brain urges for more" (Cardwell, E., 2019) via dopamine release (through visual stimulation and/or masturbation). Also contributing to the problem is that technology on our phones, ipads, or computers is readily available.

Case in point is my own perpetrator who sat in prison while my head remained attached to pornography pictures and on porn sites. One site had been taken down, but I was told by the FBI that another one or two were still active. I decided to go to that site looking for "Dana the MILF"… (sorry I won't be sharing those vile sites). I found a lot of "Dana"s, but not me.

One person (Dana) was in fact a porn star and had numerous short videos of her having sex, primarily anal intercourse. I admit I went through all the short videos or pictures just on the one title - something about her fantasy sex life. I think there were at least 100 short porn videos, along with numerous pictures. I couldn't believe with one swipe to this website I had things I could see which my mind couldn't have come up with. My daughter was down from college and I did show her some of the exerts, she noted, "Mom that's disgusting get off that shit!" I just wanted her to know what males her age are looking at and how they may be objectifying women or young girls these days.

In the deep part of the brain the excitement that porn brings is similar to an illicit drug because the reward circuits are strengthened. When

Dana Shepard-Cardwell, M.Ed.

something feels good it is imprinted in the brain's reward system. This is why cocaine is an addictive drug. The body and mind want more of the pleasure principle, the dopamine circuit gets rewired. A similar thing takes place with internet porn. A good YouTube video from Christopher Harris titled "Dopamine and the frontal lobes" describes the reward channels related to dopamine. Several other YouTube videos include: "Your Brain on Porn", "Why Porn Changes the Brain", "Part 1: Introduction Your Brain on Porn", "Part 2: The Coolidge Effect, Your Brain on Porn", "The Great Porn Experiment by Gary Wilson", "Your Brain on Porn by Gary Wilson".

I must say after looking through the porn videos and pictures, my mind felt different, kind of hyper-aroused and hyperactive, but not all too excited. It was more like when you pass a major car accident and you feel you should look to see what happened, but you know it's not a good thing if you see people laying in the median hurt with blood all over them? Yet, you look and may become disturbed later? That's how I felt. Like I had to see what was behind the next door, the swiping left to see what's next?

So how does ejaculation specifically release endorphins? Ejaculation fills the dendrites of dopamine, serotonin, GABA, and norepinephrine receptors. Wow!! That's better than most drugs, which may target only a few of those receptors. No wonder porn is so addicting.

How many guys do you know who only watch porn? People don't usually just "watch". Masturbation or sex afterwards usually goes with porn viewing. The website Your brain on porn noted "desensitization is just one of many brain changes caused by porn addiction." A few others include sensitization (forming false memory circuits to reinforce the addiction, like Pavlovian rewards), hypo-frontality (weakening of the impulse control circuits), and dysfunctional stress circuits (stress will easily trigger a need to relapse to the addiction). The website strongly recommends watching, Your Brain on Porn: Porn Addiction (2015). I also have the book, Your Brain on Porn which is so informative.

You may wonder, "How does a person go from plain vanilla soft porn to more graphic, vulgar, extreme scenes?" "Desensitization is behind tolerance, which is the need for greater and greater stimulation to experience the same high. Porn users often escalate to new genres to jack up their lagging dopamine. Studies supported the fact that fewer

65

Dana Shepard-Cardwell, M.Ed.

nerve connections were the result of reduced grey matter in the reward related region of porn addicts. In a sense, they killed some of their nerve cells related to the reward circuit and need a higher dose to activate the sluggish neurons. (www.yourbrainonporn.com) One researcher, Simone Kuhn noted that regular use of pornography could wear out your natural reward system.

It's like that car wreck scene. How many of us drive by and not look? You don't. You look. But then you can't unsee it and it's stuck in your mind. It stays in the limbic area due to having an emotional connection. The same with porn once you see the car wreck, you want a train wreck, then an airplane wreck, then you may gravitate to rape scenes, incest, transgender sex, just like that. It's an emotional tie that wants more to see more of what is out there, what is the most extreme scene I can see?

Fortunately, with real life accidents there is not a sexual response, but with the internet pornography there is. However, storm chasers do get excited and that becomes like an arousal or rush, too. It's an emotional tie that can bind you. It becomes a noose. As you know, a noose binds closer the more it is drawn. Furthermore, you are hanging yourself the more you keep watching. When does porn addiction transfer over to other parts of society?

A recent study in JAMA shared the association of sexual harassment and/or sexual assault with midlife women's mental and physical health. The results found:
"Sexual harassment and sexual assault are prevalent experiences among midlife women. Sexual harassment was associated with higher blood pressure and poorer sleep. Sexual assault was associated with poorer mental health (depression & anxiety) and sleep. Efforts to improve women's health should target sexual harassment and assault prevention." (JAMA Internal Medicine. 2019; 179(1):48-53, doi:10.1001/ jamainternmed.2018.4886)

I suspect many women in this study have been, also, exposed to sexual assault or violence at a younger age; it's a travesty that they are still dealing with problems later in life resulting in continued mental health issues of depression and anxiety and physical issues associated with high blood pressure and insomnia.

SECRETS…..

Dana Shepard-Cardwell, M.Ed.

The word angry in Greek means "to burn".

Sin or the idea of sin appeared in the first book of the Bible, Genesis. Eve "saw that the tree was good." She got drawn into something purely with her sight. She became enticed with the beauty of the tree and it's amazingly stunning fruit. Eve saw that it was "desirable to make one wise" and then what did she do?

Did she walk away?
No, she became impulsive and consumed with possessing the very thing she was told to stay away from - the fruit. "She took of its fruit and ate." To make matters worse, she convinced her partner, Adam, to partake.

Immediately after doing something wrong, "Adam and his wife hid themselves from the presence of the Lord God" (v8).

This was the beginning of sin and secrets. Both will destroy your life. Sin becomes a pattern, a way of life. And how many people talk openly about their sins? How many people come up to you and say, "Hey, I just took money from my grandmother?" or "Hey, I just snorted a gram of cocaine?" or "Hey, I just looked at porn for an hour?" Sin becomes a pattern in your life, a way of life. This leads to a life of secrets, of sweeping the trash or filth under the rug.

We cannot live a healthy lifestyle in this way. In fact, we can eat all the right foods, follow a strict diet, and look healthy on the outside, but with sin and secrets we are killing our souls on the inside. The inside of your body becomes consumed with a plague that ends up destroying you. Clean your mind, body, and soul by washing away those impurities that burn inside you. How can you do that? By letting go of secrets and working on changing the sin in your life.

Revelation 21:8
"But cowards, those who refuse to believe, who do evil things, who kill, who sin sexually, who do evil magic who worship idols and tell lies - all these will have a place in the lake of burning sulfur. This is the second death."

Iron Nugget: Confession time. What secrets do you need to release? What sins do you need to wash away?

Dana Shepard-Cardwell, M.Ed.

The PIED Piper…..

Back to the internet pornography study wondering if it was causing sexual dysfunction. The authors cited a 2014 study of new diagnoses of ED, erectile dysfunction, in active duty servicemen from 2004 to 2013 which had more than doubled. The cross sectional study of active duty males aged 21-40 found an overall ED rate of 33%. It also noted underreporting of service men due to stigmatization and biases. Another study in 2015 found men (mean age 36) who had ED accompanied by low desire for partnered sex were seeking help for their excessive use of pornography to masturbate. Furthermore, another study in 2015, "Brief Communication" reported ED rates as high as 31% in sexually active men and low sexual desire rates as high as 37%. Traditionally, the authors noted, ED has been an age related problem as one gets older. ED issues under 40 may have been related to drug and alcohol addictions, morbid obesity, or other health diseases, in the past, but only at a very small percentage of males.

One study by Kinsey Institute researchers in 2007 were among the first to report pornography related ED (PIED). They also reported pornography induced low libido. Half of the subjects were recruited from bars and bathhouses. Around half of the participants were unable to achieve erections with mild visual stimulation. The researchers found that high exposure to pornography videos resulted in lower response and "an increased need for more extreme specialized or kinky material to become aroused."

"Since the evidence had mounted that internet pornography may be a factor in the rapid surge in rates of sexual dysfunction. Nearly 6 out of 10 of the 4,000 visitors seeking help on the www.medhelp.org ED forum, who mentioned their ages were younger than 25." The comments left from participants on this website noted the word "porn" appeared most frequently. Another study in 2015 of men (avg age 41) seeking treatment for hyper-sexuality, who masturbated 7 or more hours per week, found that 71% had sexual dysfunctions, of those 33% had difficulty orgasming.

"A 2014 functional magnetic resonance imaging (fMRI) study, with compulsive internet pornography users (avg age 25) whose brains were scanned for evidence of addiction, reported they had less libido or erectile function with partnered sex, but not having erectile issues with sexually explicit material." Furthermore, two studies in 2016 with couples concluded that the marriages most negatively affected

68

were those of men who were viewing pornography at the highest frequencies, once or more times a day. Some of the men reported going from pornography use to help arousal with their partner to more explicit needs to online sexual activities with an unknown partner.

Porn addictions increase cravings, that is why a proper diet is not just needed with recovery, it's necessary and that along with the right exercise could be a cure for the addiction. No soda. Limited alcohol if one is not an alcoholic. Limited caffeine, like 1-2 cups of coffee a day. Limit nicotine, which throws the body off balance, if addicted to nicotine you may find a CBT vape to replace the nicotine and calm the nerves. Homeostasis is the goal and moderation is key related to diet. Sometimes meds are needed, but then again in moderation, not excess of being over medicated, which is just as dangerous.

An interesting verse in Proverbs 4:14 notes, "Enter not into the path of the wicked, and go not the way of evil men." It's a pretty simple message that there is good and evil that exists in this world. There are those who have been hurt and those who hurt people, and then there are those that want to get better and those who do not or will not get help. Our mission should be to align with healthy, honest, and good connections. In my field of mental health, I'm willing to help those who want help, but those who don't want help are usually referred elsewhere. I'm not there to spin in circles on the hamster wheel and I'm not there to help a person who refuses to change or look at themselves honestly.

As noted, "Your Brain on Porn", also found many of the men who watched porn or masturbate to porn daily became addicted and eventually developed sexual dysfunction issues with real partners from Erectile dysfunction, to loss of libido, to Premature ejaculation, delayed ejaculation, and anorgasmia (inability to orgasm). There has only been one cure thus far for porn addiction. That's a reboot and giving up all internet porn all together. This has been shown to be successful, but in the meantime some experience "flat line" and that's a flaccid, dead cock. The reboot takes anywhere from a few months to half a year to a year, depending on the person. One must remember if they want to be cured, there's no buffet line, no just a little bit of porn. It's cold turkey. Look for a therapist and yoga instructor, along with acupuncture to help you through this difficult time.

Dana Shepard-Cardwell, M.Ed.

A 2017 Cybersex addiction rate study reported that 19%, 1 in 5, college age men were addicted to porn, while less than 4% of women were. Some other studies related to porn use have found addiction rates averaging around 25% for male users. Young male teens who find themselves addicted to pornography often have co-morbidities of social anxiety, depression, or suicidal ideations even though they thought porn was a solution to their problems, rather than a source of their problems. Some teens believe that regular masturbation will prevent cancer, so over-use, sexual dysfunction, and addiction become a streamlined diagnosis rather than a cancer preventative.

Porn use tends to be a dirty little secret, so it makes sense that young male virgins are not even aware of the fire they are playing with, which then spreads into a wild fire or mental disorders and sexual dysfunctions. Fortunately, internet porn addiction and the sexual dysfunctions that go with them are easily cured with abstinence. On the opposite spectrum, unfortunately, most clinicians and doctors don't know about porn addiction and too many males end up with medications and diagnosis related to anxiety, depression, low testosterone, ADHD (concentration issues), low self esteem, and OCD. An informative YouTube video on rebooting is "How long will it take to reboot my brain from porn?".

Typically, if the male does bring up issues of inability to get an erection or climax with their partners, the doctor labels it performance anxiety or low T. Some leave with a shot of testosterone and others leave with a prescription of the little blue pill, Viagra. Hopefully, the doctor will order lab work related to testosterone levels and not just give a shot of testosterone.

One 25 year old woman and her 35 year old boyfriend I saw complained of his inability to perform or his lack of desire due to low T. With further investigation, he was in the oilfield and spent weeks away from her attached to his computer and watching porn during the evenings. She couldn't figure out why he would have her send body shots (nudes) of her when he was away, but when he came home he wasn't interested in sex with her or had a hard time getting an erection. He blamed it on low T, until I informed her of the PIED phenomena.

Some young males have become perverted with the need for fetish or illegal porn that they start having suicidal ideations from fear of never

Dana Shepard-Cardwell, M.Ed.

having a normal, vanilla sex life. These young males have no idea that a good psychotherapist and going cold turkey off porn will allow them to eventually resume a normal sex life. Disturbingly, "An Oxford University study found that moderate or severe addiction to the internet was associated with increased risk for self harm" (Your Brain on Porn).

Another 20 something female I saw in therapy, who had a baby, complained of her partner's lack of sexual desire due to porn use. To further complicate matters, she found the deep fakes on his computer where he had taken her friend's face and had it posted to a porn star's nude body. He, like Chris, had gone from the porn addiction to transferring over to a cyber stalking type behavior related to her friend. My client was conscious about her weight gain after the baby. She felt his addition became worse while she was pregnant even though she wanted to resume sexual practices with him after the pregnancy.

Many of the No Fap forum users report the following issues from regular porn use: depression, anxiety, stress, low self esteem, concentration problems, loss of attraction to people, sexual dysfunctions, altered sexual tastes, dissatisfaction with regular sex, conflict in relationships, lack of hygiene, increased drug use, anger, negativity, loss of interest in daily life. Many of those on the No Fap forums noted all the problems that came with porn use were eventually decreased or eliminated after recovery from the porn addiction. If you have a teen, "The Teenage Brain on Porn" found on YouTube is a very informative documentary video.

Dana Shepard-Cardwell, M.Ed.

Good Vs Evil, Id Vs Ego
And Feeling Heard

I love to collect old books and magazines. There is a wonderful, quaint antique mall in tiny Comfort, Texas on High Street where I shop. I was recently delighted to find a 1953 book on Psychiatry for medical students. Chapter 7 discusses the concept of marginal consciousness versus the repressed unconscious of Freud.

For those who are unfamiliar with Freud, he was a psychiatrist who trained with a variety of famous doctors before him, but he always seemed to part ways in a hostile manner from most of his cohorts. Freud tended to agree with a few of his colleagues at first, then drastically parted from them. The 1953 Fundamental Psychiatry book noted, "Freud was insistent on finding a cause for hysterical episodes (psychosis). The conclusion Freud reached on etiology of the neuroses (a mental and emotional disorder, less disturbing than psychosis) may be best stated in his own words, 'I now learned from my rapidly increasing experience that it was not any kind of emotional excitation that was in action behind this phenomena of the neurosis but habitually one of a sexual nature, whether it was a current sexual conflict or the effect of earlier experiences." (p. 60)

The book goes on to share, "For Freud the question of etiology of the neuroses was settled by his conclusion it could all be traced to sex." Unfortunately, many jumped on this bandwagon and treatment took a nosedive for those who treated patients and believed all mental and emotional disorders had an unconscious sexual issue. Freud went from touching people's foreheads to increase forgotten memories, to using word associations, to analyzing their dreams. His work on the Ego, Superego, and Id do have some merit, in my opinion, but not the rest of his work.

What is interesting is Freud's own ego, he wrote:
"Jung attempted to give the facts of analysis a fresh interpretation of an abstract, impersonal and non-historical character, and thus hoped to escape the need for recognizing the importance of infantile sexuality and of the Oedipus complex as well as the necessity for any analysis of childhood. Adler seemed to depart still further from psycho-analysis; he entirely repudiated the importance of sexuality traced back the formation both of character and of the neuroses solely to men's desire for power and to their need to compensate for their

72

Dana Shepard-Cardwell, M.Ed.

constitutional inferiority, and threw all the psychological discoveries of psychoanalysis to the winds." (Fundamental Psychiatry, 1953, p 60)

Common websites share Freud's Id, Superego, and Ego in psychoanalysis as three distinct yet interacting agents of the mind. The Id is "the set of uncoordinated instinctual trends (the teenage brain), the super-ego plays the critical and moralizing role, and the ego is the organized, realistic part that mediates between the desires of the id and the super-ego." The Wikipedia site says, "The superego is observable in how someone can view themselves as guilty, bad, shameful, weak, and feel compelled to do certain things." Four general levels are found in Freud's work, "the auto-erotic, the narcissistic, the anal, and the phallic." Personally, I think Freud's work was a characteristic of a truly disturbed doctor who brought his own subconscious to light and tried to make many of us re-victimized. I think if you buy into a current theme, you may get duped and find out the product they are selling or service that is supposed to be all that, really isn't.

There was an appendix in the 1953 Fundamental Psychiatry related to Freud's pansexualism (relating to or characterized by sexual desire or sexual attraction) by the Sovereign Pontiff (the Pope) in an address to the First International Congress 9/14/1952 on "The Moral Limits of Medical Research and Treatment". The Pope reported, "In order to rid himself of repression, inhibitions or psychic complexes man is not free to arouse himself for therapeutic purposes each and every appetite of a sexual order which is being excited or has been excited in his being, appetites whose impure waves flood his unconscious or subconscious mind. He cannot make them the object of his thoughts and fully conscious desires with all the shocks and repercussions such a process entails. For a man and a Christian there is a law of integrity and personal purity, of self respect, forbidding him to plunge so deeply into the world of sexual suggestions and tendencies. Here is the medical and psychotherapeutic interests of the patient to find a moral limit."

On the Pope's rebuttal of Freud's pansexualism, I say "Amen" to calling out the quackery of those hiding behind medical diagnoses and those doctors or mental health professionals using narcissism at the expense of their patients. Check out the YouTube video "How to Control Your Ego" Episode 1.

73

Dana Shepard-Cardwell, M.Ed.

Len Sperry in his book "Spirituality in Clinical Practice" (2012) shared the primary goal of spiritually oriented psychotherapy is psychological change, while its secondary goal is spiritual change or growth. Sperry has a section dedicated to the spiritual dimension and the narcissistic personality. He noted narcissistic personalities exhibit tremendous potential, but "inevitably problems arise". The Narcissistic personality types tend to experience emptiness in their relationships. Sounds a bit like Freud's own relationship issues with his close cohorts. Freud ended up distancing himself from his colleagues and he apparently thought he alone had the answers to mental neurosis, not the others.

Sperry related narcissism and evil, "evil behaving individuals attack others instead of facing their own failures; construct layers of self deception to avoid the pain of self examination, and too often, wreak havoc in the lives of others. Human evil has been described as that which kills the spiritual and has been linked to narcissism." Sperry noted various psychological definitions of evil and one by Zimbardo (2007) which defines evil as consisting of "intentionally behaving in ways that harm, abuse, demean, dehumanize, or destroy innocent others, or using one's authority and power to encourage or permit others to do so on your behalf." I think Hitler would be the prime example of the utmost evil and narcissistic human in our current history.

So, where does porn come into play with personalities; does it create evil people or narcissistic people?

Gary Wilson has numerous videos on how porn consumes the male brain. His book and website www.yourbrainonporn.com share a lot of useful information. One recent study found that pornography does lead to unethical behaviors. The results on Gary's website noted, "Consuming pornography causes individuals to be less ethical. We find that this relationship is mediated by increased moral disengagement from dehumanization of others due to viewing pornography. Combined, our results suggest that choosing to consume pornography causes individuals to behave less ethically" (Mecham,N, Lewis-Western, Wood, 2019). This study was reported in the 2019 Journal of Business Ethics.

Dana Shepard-Cardwell, M.Ed.

Do you think people become less ethical with regular porn use? When I was sexually harassed by a Principal, as a High School teacher years ago, the Principal was actually fired due to the IT administrator's discovery that the Principal was viewing porn during school on the school issued computer. No wonder he constantly followed me and targeted me with dumb blonde jokes. On one occasion, when he grabbed me and gave me a full frontal hug, I pulled away and walked off. How can this be allowed? I couldn't believe I had to put up with a year of his disgusting crap. I was young and afraid of blowing the.. whistle. This guy even had me ride with him to look at the progress of the new school being built, then had the nerve to stop by his house to pick something up. He asked me if I wanted to come in, "No, I'll wait here.", was my response, but, "HELL NO!" was what I was thinking. Rightfully so, after hearing about his porn viewing later that year.

A survey in 2018 estimated nearly 60% of respondents watch pornography at work (McDonald, 2018). Furthermore, it was noted that 70% of all internet pornography traffic happens between 9am and 5pm. Frequently women are afraid of losing their jobs, like me, so they don't report the harassment and we become anxious and irritated when we go home for the day and take it out on our spouses. My poor husband put up with a lot back then.

Some porn or drug abusers users will recognize they've strayed off the path of righteousness and self actualization and get back on the right path. We've all taken a wrong turn at some point in our life, right? Myself included! I feel this is the case with many of the abused, aggressive, and traumatized teens I work with at a residential treatment center, RTC. I tell them the adults in their lives go astray by neglecting or abusing them, but it may not be this way forever. The addicted parent may recover and get the help they desperately need. This is where prayer and forgiveness come in. When teens have very little control over their current lives, they can control their lives with prayer. When we pray regularly for those who are lost or those who are consumed by evil, it could finally reach them and the lost could find their way back home. Like Dorothy in *The Wizard of Oz*, put on your ruby red glass slippers, click your heels together, and think it!

Dr. Harry Fisch, a urologist, who wrote, The New Naked, shared, "A man who masturbates frequently can soon develop erection problems when he is with his partner. Add porn to the mix and he can become unable to have sex." Furthermore, the book and website

75

Dana Shepard-Cardwell, M.Ed.

<u>www.yourbrainonporn</u> refer to multiple studies in the last decade which a variety of assessment tools used reported as many as 1 in 3 young men having difficulties with partnered sex due to internet use. Well, this may decrease our STD stats from a few years ago!

"In 2016 a Canadian sexologist study showed problems in sexual functioning are curiously higher in adolescent males than in adult males. Over a 2 year period, 78.6% of males ages 16-21 reported a sexual problem during partnered sex." (YourBrainonPorn) Erectile dysfunction accounted for 46% of the group and difficulty orgasming showed 24% of the problems. Young viral rats, rabbits, bulls, etc. don't have these problems, but then again, they don't have the internet either.

Studies suggest that Erectile Dysfunction leads to depression and not the other way around. Depression doesn't cause Erectile Dysfunction. Our brains are constantly changing and the only thing concrete, related to the brain, is that our brains are moldable and have plasticity. With this being noted, the "vast majority of guys need 2-6 months to fully recover from problems that arise from porn use" (<u>www.yourbrainonporn.com</u>). One young man shared on <u>www.yourbrainonporn.com</u> "I used transgender porn to get hard so I could finish with heterosexual porn. Without realizing, I was soon watching a lot of taboo and extreme porn that I never would have considered a couple of years ago. I couldn't believe I let myself get to this point. I just couldn't stop myself."

Besides God coming into play, why does therapy work when one is trying to stop porn addiction? Because the client has an interested and connected person to hear their inner thoughts, unconditionally. I figured out that life is not about talking so people will hear us. No, it's about listening so they feel heard. Dr. Deepak Chopra shares in his book "SuperBrain" although the "lower brain is still with us, generating primitive and often negative drives like fear and anger, the brain is constantly evolving. The new field of positive psychology is teaching us how to best use free will to promote happiness and overcome negativity." Our brain has so many different directions it can take. "Your brain contains over 100 billion neurons. Neurons project threads known as axons and dendrites which deliver both chemical and electrical signals across the synapses. A neuron contains many dendrites to receive information from other nerve cells." (Chopra, D. 2012).

Dana Shepard-Cardwell, M.Ed.

Our thoughts are responsible for delivering signals to our brains. Dr. Chopra shares that we can promote brain growth, or neuroplasticity, by exposing ourselves to new and positive experiences. The doctor and spiritual leader points out the importance of practicing positive mental exercises as much as participating in physical exercise to rewire our brains and live a happy and healthy life. "A physical workout builds muscle" improves cell regeneration and oxygen throughout the brain and body, while a positive mental workout "creates new synapses to strengthen the neural network." Therapy is a way to get a mental workout, yoga is awesome for physical and mental regeneration. Dr. Chopra goes on to note that intense emotions from childhood abuse may be suppressed and can only be retrieved with intensive therapy or hypnosis. I've found EMDR works similar to hypnosis, but with more resolve after the sessions have ended.

If you've read this far, you may recognize why so many people have hijacked minds in this modern aged Western civilization. The mind is a fascinating thing and the brain is so complex we can't just treat it with one modality, one pill, one prayer, one yoga session, one day of mediation, one EMDR session. No, our minds and brains are like our cars, they must be washed, waxed, maintained, filled full of the right gasoline (our diets) and kept in alignment for purposes of not going off the road and staying on the "highway" that will lead us to our final destinations.

Emotional stress and trauma in mice was shown to produce glucocorticoids in the brain, toxins that kill cells in the brain. The part that bothers me about Freud's view is, it is based on the negative. Dr. Chopra shares information from Daniel Siegel, a mindful psychiatrist, SIFT is a way to think during our day. S is for sensation, I is for image, F is for feeling, T is for thought. "Nothing is real except through these channels: either you sense it as a sensation (pain or pleasure), imagine it visually, feel it emotionally, or think about it." Sifting goes on constantly throughout our day. We live in a physical world with an external reality and internal reality. The problem is we allow the external to often shape how we feel internally. Just think what would have gone through your mind if you were a male patient of Freud's. You would have been like, "Oh, all my problems started with me wanting to have sex with my mother, so I need to find someone who reminds me of mom?" And then of course, have sex with her? (I'm being facetious.)

77

Dr. Siegel addresses the attachment system in his book *The Developing Mind*, he addresses what many of us have been through growing up, which is an inability to remember much of our childhood. We say it was good, but can't remember details and tend to dismiss much as if in a dissociative way. This came from a childhood where parents had a lack of emotional comfort or connection to their children. We grew up with a mental adaptation, not a conscious choice because there was a lack of attunement. For many of my early years, I wondered if I suffered from trauma, but when I looked back on the rape scene, I know I had not been previously raped. Many of us have similar experiences from lack of connection in our homes as children, which creates similar dissociative states as does abuse. Neglect is a serious issue for children which from a dismissing parent creates an avoidant child who becomes somewhat unemotional and aloof. There is hope though, we can learn to connect to others and attach later in life.

Dr. Chopra shares that for us to become integrated in body and mind, we need to be more like a baby. A baby knows what it feels, expresses it, and absorbs the environment around him. As adults, he points out that we choose denial, repression, forgetfulness, inattention, selective memory, personal bias, and old bad habits to hold us back. "You can't feel balanced, safe, happy, and in tune until you regain the wholeness that comes naturally to a baby.
Dr. Chopra notes why finding your power includes losing weight if you are overweight. "The key is to bring your brain into balance and then use its ability to balance everything; hormones, hunger, cravings, habits. Use your brain, don't let it use you. Make new neural networks. When a person fights the urge to overeat, the brain is remembering that overeating is what it is supposed to do."

Yoga and meditation are valuable ways to lose weight and create a super brain through new neural networks. I often use yoga and meditation to help facilitate the grounding process before, during, and after using EMDR in therapy. Most of my clients know it works, but they don't recognize how they are building new neural networks to heal and repair the damaged and stressed networks.

Dana Shepard-Cardwell, M.Ed.

STRESS!!!

Dr. Gregg Henriques in his article "The Root of Suffering" conveys that stress and "a neurotic temperament sets the stage for trouble, the root of much long-term suffering takes hold when individuals battle with themselves developing negative reactions to their negative feelings."

Young people are putting more stress on their developing brains through internet use. Females with social media like Facebook, Instagram, and Snapchat and males through violent games and pornography. Young males are training their brains whether they are conscious about it or not. When the developing brain is consistently exposed to violence, porn, or drugs, it becomes altered from the average teen brain. It becomes rewired and not in a good way!

For young males, this can lead to unusual fetishes which then leads to becoming disturbed and confused with their urges. Teens and those with ADHD tend to be "thrill seekers". If you give an 18 year old a Porsche 911, do you think he'll actually go the speed limit? So, when you open up all these visual channels to porn for free from VW bugs to Jags to military tanks, doesn't it make sense that he'll check it out? See how fast it will go from 0-60? See how powerful it is?

Some of these disturbing porn sites have fetishes for rape scenes, incest, tweens, gang sex where fetishes of ass to mouth are common. The scenes show a man pulling out of one woman's ass and another woman performs oral sex on the man directly after. Examples of this are shown on several documentaries about the porn industry on the website TopDocumentaryFilms.com. There is even a documentary on A Guide to Happiness, but related to the porn industry a good documentary to watch is Diary of a Porn Virgin which follows two women who break into the industry.

Another documentary on the website is "Porndemic" which examines the epidemic of porn addiction including teenage cell phone users. This documentary also "speaks to law and order experts who think that obscenity on the internet is out of control and beyond the law, and to the blandly confident businessmen who are the new faces of corporate, mainstream porn."

Personally, I feel our minds have become hijacked and similar to the ancient Sodom and Gomorrah. Whatever your "thing" is, from eating too much sugar, to drinking too much wine, to constantly looking at FB/SnapChat/ Twitter/Instagram, to porn, to video games, to internet shopping, to collecting material things, to expensive cars, etc. When will our time come up? When will we be consumed by our own desires resulting in nefarious STDS, HPV, cancer (from genetically altered foods and too much sugar), too much alcohol, too little exercise? Have you considered how your own lifestyle is affecting how you live? The choices that you make which affect your mind and your body?

When will we open our eyes to recognize how we cause most of our mental and physical health issues? Why do we tend to wait until it's too late? Until our minds have become consumed with depression, anxiety, obsessions, and dirty little secrets which cause so much stress? Until our bodies revolt on us with discomfort and pain and we go to the doctor to get 1, 2, 3, 4 maybe more band-aides in the form of Western medication, pills, which only cover up what festers below the skin. Secrets lead to stress and then to misery, which is what the pharmaceutical companies bank on. The American system thrives on our secrets.

It's time for us to wake up. Private information is constantly shared and judged by companies to profit off of you. Money truly is the root of most evil. Pharmaceuticals and the sex industry are two of the top money making industries in the U.S. and are causing us stress that kills us! Many of the psychotropic meds have side effects a mile long. I know, personally speaking, I'm still having brain farts, holes in my thinking, from too many years of taking antidepressants. I finally don't feel like a zombie or numb from the pills, but the withdrawal left me with huge concentration problems. At the time of finishing up this book, I'm on a quest after watching another documentary, *The Reality of Truth*. Please, check it out on You Tube.

To add to our stress, Big Brother is not as safe as you many think. A friend noted in 1994 that his father worked for the Pentagon, Ironically this guy's nickname was "Mullet", but he shared information back then that the government had eyes on most everyone in the U.S. at one point in time or another. Edward Snowden proved this later in 2013 when he leaked classified info from the National Security Agency while he was an employee for the CIA. Lobbyists

Dana Shepard-Cardwell, M.Ed.

also have their eyes on you and their hands in your politicians' pockets. My favorite saying was found on a bumper sticker years ago, "Politicians like dirty diapers should be changed periodically and for the same reasons." This became my mantra for a while. Maybe we should make it the national anthem?

Google CEO, Eric Schmidt, shared, "If you have something you don't want someone to know, then maybe you shouldn't be doing it in the first place." Legit!!! I remember a friend who dated a doctor who had a weird fetish.. dressing up like a gorilla and chasing her around before sex…. Or maybe it was just acting like a gorilla and beating his chest and chasing her around, can't recall specifics? Regardless, she spilled the beans during a girls' night, we laughed, and now whenever I see him around town I think about doc as the gorilla. If she were a little younger, that Monkey Business would have been posted and public. At least only a few of us "mature" ladies laugh out loud about him. This is an example of word of mouth, but Google shares your fetishes, your searches, and that folks, spreads like wild fires. Your Monkey Business becomes public!

Stress can consume our lives, just like addictions. Tamsen Butler on her blog, gives us 101 Stress Relievers after noting that Yale University research "reveals a correlation between stress and chronic physical conditions."

Google shares your medical searches, your mental health searches, and even your sex searches. Have you read the 15 page terms and conditions of most websites? NOT! We want immediate gratification, so we just click and "agree" to get on our merry way. The same with our food choices. Fast quick, genetically modified foods which lead to the fact that 70% of the U.S. is now obese. We go for the enticingly tasting foods which alter our taste buds, no different than how porn alters our visual neurons.

Due to altered foods, cancer is running rampant and our sugar consumption is out of the roof. I know family members who say they are hypoglycemic yet consume so much sugar laden food that they should be in a coma. I truly am hypoglycemic and can barely tolerate my 80% pure cocoa at night. My addictions are red wine and dark chocolate. On cruises, I tend to indulge in cocktails and desserts, but pay the price while lying in bed moaning and groaning. My daughter and husband pay a higher price at having to put up with me and fuss

81

Dana Shepard-Cardwell, M.Ed.

at me for making bad choices. (I did just this while cruising alone and drinking 3 Bahama Mamas in Nassau. I had a migraine for 3-4 hours and had to lie down until it passed. Thank goodness it was during the day and not time to go to bed.)

We cause more stress by eating so much sugar or processed foods which lead to depression and anxiety. Many of these foods create blood sugar issues which affect our moods from excitement, to anger, to lethargy, to hyper-activity, to depression and anxiety. Our bodies are in constant dis-ease with the current American food system. Now take away the hyphen in that word. This is our state. Hippocrates saw into the future: "Let thy food be thy medicine and medicine be thy food", 400 BC. Hippocrates emphasized the importance of nutrition to prevent or cure disease. Even Socrates was wise before his time. He recognized the Idiotites, idiots.

Our current Western medical model is micromanaged and hijacked by the pharmaceutical companies. Why do you think natural products like broccoli and strawberries can't be patented or FDA approved? Because they are natural God made food.. From Socrates, "To move the world, we must first move ourselves. Strong minds discuss ideas, average minds discuss events, weak minds discuss people."

The time of Hunger Games and Divergent are here, folks. Society is divided into factions. The only difference is that we are being controlled by the media as one faction, the pharmaceutical companies, the food industry, the government and politicians. Oh, you fools are blind. It's not a Black Lives matter against White Supremacy issue at all!! It's the billion dollar industries that wreck our lives that create turmoil, cancer, distress, crime, hate, anger, false realities. We have allowed these fools to take over our minds and our bodies. The Evil is Real, yet you choose to close your eyes to what lies in front of you.

Dr. Henriques tells his readers that it's not the crime, but the cover up that harms you. "This secondary negative reaction to the original feelings often creates a vicious cycle that results in major depression and generalized anxiety disorder." There is help, though. You don't have to sulk in all those negative thoughts and you can choose to rise up against the factions that control your life.

Socrates pointed out that through a process of questioning, the soul can be brought to remember the ideas in their pure form, thus

Dana Shepard-Cardwell, M.Ed.

bringing wisdom. When have you last questioned your current life, your direction, who you are, the "what if's" in your life? Or do you sit idle or stuck in your current situation complaining about your job, your spouse and why the job you applied for hasn't called you? This reminds me of a recent conversation with a friend. It didn't go well when I brought up numerous questions. She got very defensive and walked off from the dinner table. Unfortunately, I couldn't feel sorry for her.

The "Ego" tends to try and control us through judgement, over-planning, and defense mechanisms. By learning to let go and find positive coping tools we can continue to grow and embrace life. We gain the ability to trust again. Not everyone is dangerous, not everyone is out to harm us. There are good people in the world. Technology ends up leading to more Ego problems. David Levy, who used to work for Google recognized the dangers of technology and left the tech field to help people. He wrote a book titled, *Mindful Tech: How to bring balance to our digital lives.*

One client recently noted she puts up a wall and doesn't allow herself to trust anyone, because she has had so many assaults in her life. We are working on bringing down the walls of fear and shame in her life, so she can lead a productive life. This woman had years of drug abuse, stemming from trauma she received as a child. Once she got into the drug world, this led to another chain of continued abuse by drug induced offenders.

As Dr. Daniel Siegel pointed out in an article on neurobiology of the developing mind, "Energy and information can flow within one brain or between brains. In this manner, the ways in which energy and information flow within an individual or between two individuals helps create the experience of the mind." This is why many times those exposed to early trauma become victims later in life as they are drawn to the trauma dance to which they've grown accustomed. Drug addicts are not your friends; they never will be while they are under the influence. They use charisma to entice your mind to want to believe their bullshit. But that's all it will ever be; a pile of poop.

Research shows the availability, potency, and the addictive nature of narcotics has led to the worst opioid travesty in U.S. history, it continues to kill hundreds of thousands of people. (www.nytimes.com/2017/01/06/us/opiod-crisis-epidemic) The

Dana Shepard-Cardwell, M.Ed.

CDC.gov noted, the death rate from opioids increased by 72.2% in a single year from 2014-2015.

Psychology Today (2/2019) shared in the article, "Seeing Beyond Depression", "The most significant source of inflammation causing major depressive disorder is likely stress." They go on to report, "Social stress is the single biggest risk factor for depression. Major life events like bereavement, divorce, loss of employment, as well as burdensome roles increase the risk of depression weeks, months, or years later. Childhood stresses, like early separation from parents, are also predictive of depression decades later." The article refers to a New Zealand study of children which showed "The immune system's memory may mediate the link between childhood adversity and adult depression."

Most studies support the idea that it takes 30 days to establish change in our lives if we are working on developing a good habit. If it's exercise working out 3x a week for a month will most likely help develop a habit. If it's eliminating alcohol or adding fruits and veggies, then the same thing, 30 days. Maybe that's why there are 40 days in Lent? It helps us establish a change. Like giving up certain videos, certain foods, certain drinks, etc. Look at the scripture, "Why have you despised the commandment of the Lord to do evil in his sight?" 2 Samuel 12:9

I'm reminded of how David in the Bible, "fastened" his attention on the woman bathing (she didn't know he was there watching) and how his visual (filled with dopamine) turned to lust. After he did wrong, David didn't want anyone to know, so he murdered Bathsheba's husband. Was he thinking the problem would just go away?
God punished David by taking the child which Bathsheba bore, until David repented and changed. God noted, "For thou didst it secretly; but I will do this thing before all Israel, and before the sun." 2 Samuel 12:12

When we lie, or cover up the lie, we are constantly reminded of the lie/cover up and we look over our shoulders with unproductive hope. Our own deceit to fool ourselves leads to a downward spiral in our lives. Our internal and external deception becomes a volcano in our lives that could erupt like the ancient city of Pompei at any moment.

Dana Shepard-Cardwell, M.Ed.

I wonder if Chris' (my perp) unproductive hope of "being with the girls I could never be with" (his own self-fulfilling prophecy) which turned to illicit desires and drug abuse, led to any real satisfaction in his life? His addictions led to desires of the flesh, his sins to momentary pleasures which didn't appear to be worth it by spending 1.5 years in the state penitentiary and now looking at federal time waiting trial by the FBI at the federal holding jail in Bexar County for the last 9 months. So, now Chris has a criminal record and is surrounded by people ten times more dangerous than him.

Here's how the self-fulfilling prophecy works. It can be something you say or believe about yourself or something someone else has said about you. For example, you may have had a parent that called you "retarded" or a teacher that called you "stupid" when you were young. You could take little actions at school to be a good student or cause your own demise by failing or even dropping out, just because someone labeled you and you ended up accepting that belief, usually without being aware of the curse. The same is true with Chris thinking certain girls would never be with him. He ended up being alone with only his internet porn due to his own self-fulfilling beliefs. Our mind is a terrible thing to waste. In Chris' case he wasted his life and will never have children of his own most likely due to his age and an upcoming sentence.

People can't hide from God or Big Brother these days. God's moral laws are there and he sees our moods, our hearts, our souls, our actions. Wouldn't it make sense to live our lives justly and by pleasing God, not our evil advisory, the devil? When we lie to ourselves or use self- rationalization we please the devil and give him more power over our lives.

A doctor or therapist can help us heal what ails us with proper guidance and direction. God does the same on the moral level. By listening to God and doing what he guides us to do, we can become healthy, productive, and truly happy people. Things will arise that are out of our control, i.e. Chris and his cyber stalking crime toward me, but because I worked through my own self-rationalization in my past, I was able to deal with his crime in a God-filled direction. I moved through the stalking, crime, problem, etc. and turned the re-victimization into a productive tool to educate people about the dangers of pornography. I got certified as a porn addiction specialist.

85

Dana Shepard-Cardwell, M.Ed.

The interesting part is I had another stalker, who came to my yoga classes, sent me nudes, stripped down to his banana hammock underwear in my yoga class and requested I teach him nude yoga. When I blocked him on FB, he Instant Messaged me at all hours of the day. The ironic part, I was getting weird texts from this guy on the same day the FBI notified me they had charged Chris with 11 counts of cyber stalking with intent to cause harm. I found out how to block the other guy from IM.

This other "weirdo" had written me a letter a year ago when I told him not to come to my yoga class anymore or I would have to call the police to remove him and get a restraining order. His letter talked about his porn addiction and that he decided to get help for it. Obviously, he didn't get much help or relapsed because he somehow got back in touch with me by finding a way to communicate via Instant Message, even though I had deleted him from FB. Folks, I won't go into detail about "Odd Bill Hitchcock" which is my name for him, but this is another incident where a person who is a little odd, gets a hold of porn and starts stalking others. We desperately need to talk about the porn subject, because people need help. Without the help, they need, they may become dangerous.

In EMDR, the Adaptive Information Processing suggests that there are an average of 100 billion neurons in the brain. Each neuron can take 1,000 to 10,000 different directions through the synapse. What happens with traumatic events, whether little traumatic events for BIG traumatic events, "the memories with disturbing effects and sensations get dys-functionally stored and are unable to connect to other positive life experiences which are stored in other networks in the brain" (*New Notes on Adaptive Information Processing*, Francine Shapiro). The treatment approach we use in EMDR targets past experiences, current triggers, and potential future challenges to resolve the maladaptive encoding of incomplete processing resulting from the trauma or disturbing life experiences. I call this "Recovering the Hijacked Mind" (Cardwell, D. 2018).

I recently completed an "EMDR Therapy and the Treatment of Substance and Behavioral Addictions" workshop with H. Payson and K. Becker. The presenters pointed out that "The issue isn't the power of the product; it's the power of the pain." They shared several great videos, one called "The Recovering Community Movie.com" and another by Johann Hari called "Chasing the Scream". In "Chasing the

86

Dana Shepard-Cardwell, M.Ed.

Scream" it is noted that the brain likes to chase things that "almost" work. It's the excitement, or dopamine's fault.

In therapy, we look at the Adverse Childhood Experiences to recognize why many Americans have food, drug, alcohol, or behavioral addictions like porn. Compulsive behaviors rewire the brain. The longer the use, the more the brain has changed. Our hijacked minds determine our human behaviors. It doesn't really matter what the problem is related to addiction, it's a problem with dopamine! This is why intervention is needed by someone who understands the reasons behind addition and ways to help the addict, whether it be substances or behaviors.

About Wild Bill Hitchcock, he is known around town because he rides his bike everywhere. He also rings the bell for the Salvation Army at Christmas, which is scary because he is around young girls then. He's in his 40s and can't drive because of a head injury incurred years ago. Talking to him you know he's a little "off" and most of us just say social niceties to him when he walks up to start conversation, which are awkward. The problem is he may have never gotten help for his TBI, traumatic brain injury, related to social norms and processing skills. But, he's healthy enough to enjoy porn, evidently.

Wild Bill should be able to get more direction as to what is right and what is wrong. When he sent me a naked FB picture years ago, I scolded him and told him he can't do that, it's not proper behavior. I knew he was odd, so I tried to educate him. I also blocked him and then when he apologized and appeared to change a few years later, I allowed him contact again on FB. Nope, little did I know he hadn't changed, which led him to take my yoga class and become kind of "stalkerish". It was after that I had to threaten him with the police if he didn't leave me alone. He listened and wrote me the letter about his problems with porn and that he was seeing a counselor, but a year later he found a way to communicate via text, until I blocked him, again. This is an example of how some people don't appear to learn and stay connected to the addiction of porn, which transfers over to criminal type behaviors. In my case with two men in town, stalking. One cyber stalked me and the other followed me to yoga class and via texting etc. Bill even called the owner of the yoga studio one New Year's Eve requesting a private session with me. She called me and I told her "NO! That's the weird stalker guy!" She had no idea who he

87

Dana Shepard-Cardwell, M.Ed.

was. She just thought someone wanted to learn yoga from me, privately!

Try disconnecting and communing with nature this week.
Quiz Question: What are some of the medications prescribed for ADHD?
Stimulants include Adderall, Dexedrine, ProCenta, Vyvanse, Ritalin, Metadate, Concerta. The atomoxetine kind includes Strattera, and Alpha agonists include Guanfacine (Intuniv) and Clonidine (Catapres).
There is a booklet to download on medications from the National Institute of Mental Health (NIMH) that is called Mental Health Medications. You can also look up information on mental health issues from this website.

Dana Shepard-Cardwell, M.Ed.

A Pill for Every Problem.

"Where you thought your friends were just having normal troubles, the developers of the American Psychiatric Association's diagnostic bible raise the possibility that you are surrounded by the mentally ill. Equally disconcerting to you, you may be among them" (Kutchins, Kirk 97). In their book, "Making Us Crazy", Kutchins and Kirk note not sleeping can earn you a label of major depressive disorder, bearing grudges and you can look like a personality disorder, being alone and isolating can have you labeled as another personality disorder, lack of sexual interest and you can be labeled as hypoactive sexual desire disorder, worrying and you get slapped with a general anxiety disorder. All of these disorders can be medicated. It appears we are being medicated for any, and all, life situations that can possibly be thought of.

I was amazed and impressed by the film "Brain on Fire " written by Gerard Barrett and based on Susannah Cahalan's memoir, "Brain on Fire: My month of Madness". Susannah poignantly described her descent from normal to receiving numerous labels of bipolar to drug addicted to schizophrenic when all along she had a serious autoimmune disorder that could have left her dead or in a mental institution for the rest of her life if Dr. Souhel Najjar had not agreed to take over the case. All other doctors involved had failed Susannah and just prescribed one psychotropic med after the other, which obviously didn't work, and left her catatonic. Her brain was on fire from anti-MDA receptor encephalitis. She was able to fully recover her cognitive abilities, after proper diagnosis that was physical, not mental.

A report from CBS news noted in 2013 that 70% of Americans take prescription drugs. What are the most common prescriptions given to Americans? Antibiotics, thyroid medications, pain killers, and antidepressants. To top it off the report found that 20% of the U.S. patients were on 5 or more scripted meds. This is a travesty friends. Another report from a medical site noted that antidepressants were the 2nd most common prescriptions given to Americans after narcotics. The report noted from 1997 to 2016 the CDC found an 85% increase in prescription meds.

Furthermore, WebMd told its readers that many of the pills prescribed may be unnecessary and might do more harm than good. I've seen

89

Dana Shepard-Cardwell, M.Ed.

this as the case over and over in my practice with teens and children prescribed antidepressants, mood stabilizers, and ADHD meds. Remember the young boy who was switched from ADHD meds to a mood stabilizer and then started saying he wished he were dead and started banging his head on the window of the car? The doctor noted the mood stabilizer the boy was on could make "depression worse for a few patients", but never warned the mother when he first changed the boy's medication. The pediatrician only told her after she came in because I had recommended inpatient for the boy to get medication from a proper psychiatrist and watched for medication management.

On the Integrated MedFacts module given to those who take Adderall it reads, "A very bad and sometimes deadly health problem called serotonin syndrome may happen if you take this drug with drugs for depression, migraines, or certain other drugs. Call your doctor right away if you have agitation, change in balance, confusion, hallucinations, fever, fast or abnormal heartbeat, flushing, muscle twitching, or stiffness, seizures, shivering or shaking, sweating, bad diarrhea, upset stomach, or throwing up, or bad headaches. This drug may affect growth in children and teens in some cases."

Dr. Chopra has a chapter dedicated to Depression in his Super Brain book. He noted depression afflicts millions and is the leading disability among Americans between age 15 and 45. He goes on to point out that the brain "is involved in full body symptoms" as it pertains to depression. "Depression typically affects the anterior cingulate cortex, involved in negative emotions, the amygdala, responsible for emotions, and the hypothalamus, involved in sex drive and appetite. He goes on to share that you can actively reprogram your own neurochemistry and no longer be enslaved to mood disorders. Dr. Chopra reported, "When depressed patients get the right psychotherapy, their brains change in a way that resembles the changes produced by drugs."

The ironic part? Many of the youth I see in foster care not only take an ADHD medication, but they also take an antidepressant, a mood stabilizer, antipsychotic, and sedative all in one day. Granted some just take 2-3 meds, but most have serotonin drugs added to their ADHD meds and look at the labels that go with the ADHD medication alone. No wonder these kids complain of their meds.

Dana Shepard-Cardwell, M.Ed.

A website on bipolar disorder (www.mdedge.com) noted that most US psychiatrists use combination therapies for bipolar like a mood stabilizer (Lithium, Divalproex) and antipsychotic (Olanzapine, Clozapine, Risperidone, Haloperidol, Aripiprazole) to quickly control mania. It goes on to report, "Using conventional antipsychotics long-term in bipolar disorder is not advisable", yet many of the patients are placed on a harmful psychotropic medication for years without titration by their physicians.

Furthermore, Dr. Rita Khoury and Dr. Elias Ghossoub (Current Psychiatry, 2019 March; 18(3)) found that "approximately 9% of all adverse drug reaction reports involving clozapine were due to seizures, 5.9% for quetiapine, 4.9% for Olanzapine, 3.68% for Risperidone, 3.2% for Haloperidol, 2.59% for Aripiprazole." The authors did note, "Overall, the evidence regarding the seizure risk associated with antipsychotics is scarce", but what if you are one of the 9% or 5% that is affected? And what are the risks when these drugs are combined with other drugs that bind to similar receptors? These drugs were not tested in combined or comorbidity cases. They were tested with the one drug and not how it reacts with other psychotropic medication.

Dr. Sy Saeed, Dr. Mutukanagaraj, and Dr. Irene Pastis showed in an evidence based review that over 7% of the adult population in the U.S. had a major depressive episode in 2017, alone. (MDedge Psychiatry, 3/01/2019). How many people are being prescribed a mood stabilizer, antipsychotic, and antidepressant all at once? How is this damaging our brains in the long run?

Some neurotransmitters that are important in psychopharmacology include: norepinephrine, dopamine, serotonin, GABA, acetylcholine, glutamate, opioid, and endocannabinoids. Most of these medications work on the autonomic nervous system and the brain. Many people prescribed psychotropic medications are noncompliant by taking more than prescribed or skipping meds if they feel better. Withdrawal from Benzos can be dangerous including: seizures, insomnia, irritability, headaches, hyperacusis, and hallucinations. The noncompliance in medication management becomes like Russian roulette.

In *Making Us Crazy* the authors share that mental conditions frequently mediate between environmental stresses and resulting

Dana Shepard-Cardwell, M.Ed.

impairments. Many of us affected by predators end up looking like the "crazy" person, instead of the other way around. This is wrong! Why in the world was I victimized a second time by the medical profession when I was raped and assaulted as a teen? Yes, I needed help, but not a pill that I was enslaved to 2x a day for 23 years.

I tried to break free from my slavery 7 years in to the process, but under medical guidance was unsuccessful. I tried titrating on my own a couple of times, but went back to the full dose when I would get dizzy, almost faint, and have trouble concentrating. I would sweat, feel irritated, and just try to drive my vehicle without causing an accident. I finally gave in and gave up and went back to full dosage under my master, the all mighty antidepressant.

It wasn't until the shortage of my medication a few years back, that I started thinking about "What if there is a lack of my medication", "What will happen if I can't get my hands on my medication"? I can't stop cold turkey! And I wondered, "Will I be on this medication until I'm old?" All of these thoughts laid dormant for quite some time, so much so that I could have received another label of GAD, generalized anxiety disorder, which I did have in my early 30s and was given benzos for.

The benzo roller coaster was worse than the anti-depressant slavery as far as I'm concerned. Benzos work on the GABA receptors. GABA is the prominent inhibitory neurotransmitter in the CNS (central nervous system) and I involved in anxiety. Perhaps, my GABA receptors were adequately being filled, naturally? Why do doctors blindly just prescribe, not knowing what is going on with the brain? If I have stomach pains, they will take an X-Ray. Benzodiazepines would help me sleep one night, and keep me up another night, I would wake up refreshed only on a few occasions or wake up feeling lethargic and hung over on most occasions. It wasn't until I started doing yoga and deep breathing practices that I curbed the anxiety at night.

Anxiety tends to hit us more when we are trying to turn our minds off at night. During the day, we can do something different, but when left alone with our own thoughts trying to solve our problems and the world's problems. Well, this can consume a lot of hours with rumination.

92

Dana Shepard-Cardwell, M.Ed.

In one of my favorite books, *Anatomy of an Epidemic*, Robert Whitaker noted that Valium was the number one selling drug in the Western world from 1968-1981. "As people took this drug the number of people admitted to psychiatric hospitals and ERs soared." In 2007, 83 million Benzodiazepines (Valium, Xanax, etc) were prescribed in the United States, alone. Unfortunately, one trauma website noted that people frequently try to cope with their anxiety by using unhealthy patterns of avoidance" which in my opinion leads to them looking for a pill to cure the pain. A pill will not cure our pain, it will only mask the problem with a bandage.

Psychotropic medication kept me from doing the things that were working for me in the past, like exercise, the meds led to weight gain, poor eating choices, lack of socializing, not able to do endurance sports, unmotivated, etc. Here is a list of Symptoms of SSRI withdrawal: dizziness, light-headedness, vertigo, fainting, shock like sensations, paresthesia (sensation of prickling/tingling on skin), anxiety, diarrhea, fatigue, instability with gait, headaches, insomnia, irritability, nausea, vomiting, tremors, and visual disturbances. These symptoms were discussed in a workshop I took for mental health professionals by a pharmacist. Common SSRIs are fluoxetine (Prozac), sertraline (Zoloft), Paroxetine (Paxil), fluvoxamine (Luvox), Citalopram (Celexa), and Escitalopram (Lexapro). The SSRIs can also be prescribed for OCD and fibromyalgia.

SSRIs deal with selective serotonin reuptake inhibitors, while SNRIs deal with serotonin and norepinephrine reuptake inhibitors. SNRIs block both 5HT and NE reuptake and include Duloxetine (Cymbalta) which is approved for depression and anxiety, along with fibromyalgia and chronic pain, Venlafaxine (Effexor), desvenlafaxine (Pristiq), milnacipran (Savalla), and levomilnacipran (Fetzima). The SNRIs tend to have more difficulties with withdrawal than the SSRIs. Atypical antidepressants may or may not block catecholamine uptake and include: bupropion (Wellbutrin, Zyban), mirtazapine (Remeron), trazodone (Oleptro) which can be sedating and used for insomnia. I've seen many adolescents prescribed antidepressants, mood stabilizers, and atypicals like trazodone for sleep at night. Other psycho-pharmaceuticals are given for treatment resistant major depressive disorder like: Olanzapine (Zyprexa), Aripiprazole (Abilify), Quetiapine (Seroquel), and Brexpiprazole (Rexulti). These are used in combination with antidepressants, often. Abilify was noted by the pharmacists as the largest selling drug in the United

States! Abilify has associated with it an increase in impulsive behavior.

More Atypical Antipsychotic pharmaceuticals include: Clozapine (Clozaril), Risperidone (Risperdal), Ziprasidone (Geodon), Asenapine (Saphris), Iloperidone (Fanapt), Lurasidone (Latuda), Paliperidone (Invega), and Cariprazine (Vraylar). Original Typical Antipsychotics, which are less used now, include: Thorazine and Haldol/Haloperidol. Some of these medications have diabetes related events, an increase for heart disease, and weight gain problems associated with them. Alternatives for lithium include: Tegretol, Depakote and valproic acid, Lamictal, Topamax, and atypical antipsychotics.

Actions in the antipsychotic drugs like Clozapine, Risperidone, Olanzapine, Aripiprazole, etc. block 5-HT receptors in the forebrain and have an additional neurochemical effect in addition to DA receptor blockage. These drugs have a sedating effect and a decrease in psychotic behavior. It's such a sad state that many of the boys in residential treatment care come with these sedating drugs to help "calm" them down. Look at the warning on many antidepressants "In clinical studies, antidepressants increased the risk of suicidal thinking and behavior in children and adolescents with depression and other psychiatric disorders." Many of the boys I have seen involved in the foster system have been to inpatient hospitals more than once for suicidal ideations.

We won't know what we're made of until we work through some struggles or until we learn how to solve some of our problems. A pill will never teach us how to solve problems, how to grow, how to survive. EMDR therapy proves that Your Own Mind has the answers, but like a flower pushing its way up from under the earth toward the sunshine, it must struggle through tough soil and dirt to become free and beautiful. You are that flower with the right therapy, exercise, and a healthy lifestyle.

Lack of exercise and eating fast foods, along with sodas and alcohol are some of the worst things for a person with depression or anxiety. Better yet, leave off exercise, eat fast foods, drink sodas and energy drinks with alcohol at night and you WILL become depressed or anxious, sooner or later.

Dana Shepard-Cardwell, M.Ed.

Dawson Church, PhD., has an awesome book, *The Genie in Your Genes*. He shares, "When looking for explanations of how the world works, we are historically more comfortable with solid objects or the use of drugs to treat disease." We are less comfortable with intangible phenomena, like electromagnetic signaling, acupuncture, EFT tapping, or the effects of consciousness and energy healing on disease. Dr. Church shares the research behind epigenetic healing, benefits of prayer, benefits of tapping, why stress leads to disease, how energy psychology works, and the power of belief therapy to change your DNA. His book is one of the most amazing pieces I've come across in a long time, along with Deepak Chopra's *Super Brain* and *Anatomy of An Epidemic* by Robert Whitaker. Three absolutely, amazing pieces of literature.

Dana Shepard-Cardwell, M.Ed.

Re-Victimized and Hijacked Minds

I wrote this to a Trouble Shooters news spot, after a recent Me Too
story:

The real crime here is the pharmacy companies who re-victimize
women. As a teen who was raped, I suffered from PTSD and
depression and went to see my doctor in my 20s. What do you think
he did? He put me on antidepressants, but never in my lifetime did I
think I would be on those pills for 20+ years. When working on my
masters in my late 20s I went to therapy, which is what helped.

A study in 2016 noted 1 in 6 Americans take a psychotropic drug
(www.scientificamerican.com). This is a travesty and the
psychotropic pharmacy companies are re-victimizing women. A
woman shouldn't have to travel around the world to find a tribal
healing center to come off the damaging effects of ant-depressants.
We should let Americans know how damaging the psychotropic
medications really are and how therapy and natural healing might be
the best choice for a large percentage of the victims out there, not a
medication that they will need to take for the rest of their lives!

I think an undercover story should be done to show how a woman in
her 20s/30s who goes to see her doctor with trauma will be prescribed
an antidepressant or even a benzodiazepine without even being
referred to a therapist, first. This re-victimizes unassuming young
women who only want to feel better, not be subjected to years of
medication which only puts a bandage on the underlying issue. This
topic needs to be addressed and uncovered, too many females are
given a pill that ends up doing more damage than the assault did!

A recent report related to "fighting the darkness" noted depression is
on the rise and "roughly 1 out of 5 women in America will experience
it in her lifetime". "Dealing with Depression" by Prevention magazine
(4/19) noted the millennials saw the largest increase in depression
diagnoses (63%) with 18-35 year old women being the second largest
increase of 47% in depression diagnoses, all reported by Blue Cross
Blue Shield. So, what appears to be making us depressed? Some say
an increase in our addiction to technology, lack of real contact, and

Dana Shepard-Cardwell, M.Ed.

the fast-paced life we live actually increases our chances of depression.

I know for myself, the trauma I suffered as a teen didn't help my situation, but it wasn't until I moved from Corpus Christi, Tx to San Antonio that things became hard to manage. I had a workout schedule in Corpus Christi which included jogging aside the ocean along the seawall and lifting weights at the local YMCA. My life had purpose and routine with friends, exercise, and eating healthy. When I moved to San Antonio to follow my fiancé who took a job there, I had no friends, no calming ocean water to jog near, and ended up eating crap to temporarily feel better, which took a downward spiral in my mental and physical health
Quiz Question: The benzodiazepine receptor is associated with a receptor complex for which neurotransmitter? Acetylcholine, Dopamine, GABA, Glutamate, Serotonin

Answer: Go back to the previous chapter to find the answer.

Natural Solutions to What Ails You

Top 10 Stress Relievers

1. Think positively. Research from the Mayo Clinic shows that thinking positively can impact stress reduction.

2. Use self-affirmation. Take time every day to compliment yourself.

3. Visualize your safe, calm place. Close your eyes and picture a calm place, a beach with blue waves and the sound of sea gulls or a mountain with a trickling stream surrounded by green ferns and a soft breeze, feel the release of tension.

4. Try yoga. This form of exercise isn't only good for your body but is good for your mind too. Yoga can relieve depression and bring a feeling of peace.

Dana Shepard-Cardwell, M.Ed.

5. Get enough sleep. Adequate sleep will help your body deal with the daily stress you encounter.

6. Learn to say no. it's time to stop agreeing to every project and invitation that comes your way.

7. Laugh. It's not only laughter that can lower the levels of stress hormones in your body, but just the anticipation of laughter can be enough according to a study at Loma Linda University.

8. Pray. Regardless of your religious beliefs, the act of praying and spending time in spiritual thought can help you deal with all the other aspects of your life. As a bonus, spiritual people may also heal faster than others, according to author Dr. Roberta Lee.

9. Listen to music. Your favorite tunes can be a great escape from stress. Listening to music for thirty minutes a day may also lower your blood pressure.

10. Vent. Instead of keeping problems bottled up inside, ask a trusted friend to listen to what is troubling you or hire a trusted therapist. Getting your problems out may help you to feel better and may also prompt you to begin thinking up solutions instead of merely simmering over the problems silently.

(Tips from Tamsen to Relieve Stress . Look for her Blog.)

Try over the counter natural amino acids like GABA for anxiety, 5-HTP for depression, Tyrosine for focus issues, St. John's Wort for depression, and products from Dr. Amen's website which combine many of the natural products to help with mood issues and, energy, concentration, depression, anxiety, etc.

"A journey of a thousand miles must begin with a single step" (Lao-Tzu).

Start with baby steps on your stress-free journey. Celebrate each morning, each afternoon, each evening. Break your days into thirds. Celebrate each day if you can put a checklist on all the thirds! Set hourly goals which will transfer over to days and before you know it your looking at weekly successes.

A few coping tools include finding a hobby, using daily meditation techniques (breathing, stretching, flow yoga), start a weekly support group, write down your feelings, distance yourself from the drama, play with an animal.

Dana Shepard-Cardwell, M.Ed.

Allow things to flow like water off of your back. Don't spend time worrying about situations that are out of your control. Use positive thinking, squash the ANTs, automatic negative thoughts. Ask for help, forgive and forget to release anger. Take one day at a time. Remember the only thing that stays the same is, Change. The world is in constant movement. This too shall pass.

"We do not sing because we are happy. We are happy because we sing" (William James, psychologist). Go out and do something to save your soul, to make a difference, to feel joy. Happiness doesn't just show up at your doorstep. Happiness is more a state of mind. A choice, no matter what hell and back you have been through. Heaven is always above and hell will always be below us. What do you choose to do: look Up or Down?

Is what you are doing in your daily life helping you? Viktor Frankl, the author of "Man's Search for Meaning" shared, "It is possible to practice the art of living even in a concentration camp, although suffering is omnipresent. The attempt to develop a sense of humor and to see things in a humorous light is some kind of trick learned while mastering the art of living." Frankl's view was that our greatest task as humans is our search for meaning no matter what conditions you are living under. "Frankl saw three possible sources for meaning: in work, in love, and in courage during difficult times. Suffering in and of itself is meaningless; we give our suffering meaning by the way we respond to it" (Harold Kushner, author of "When Bad Things Happen to Good People).

"For the meaning of life differs from man to man, from day to day and from hour to hour. What matters, therefore, is not the meaning of life in general, but rather the specific meaning of a person's life at a given moment" (Frankl).

When we live our life in the past or future we chose to live out of touch and not allow ourselves to enjoy the very moment we are in. To be afraid because something tragic happened in the past is a form of depression and to be afraid of what may happen in the future that's a form of anxiety. Live in the moment to live life to the fullest.

"It is one of the basic tenets of logotherapy that man's main concern is not to gain pleasure or to avoid pain, but rather to see a meaning in his life. We must never forget that we may find meaning in life even when confronted with a hopeless situation" (Frankl)

99

Dana Shepard-Cardwell, M.Ed.

EMDR for natural healing

Coming back from another EMDR workshop I noticed I had been frustrated due to previous doc appointments. I was dealing with trying to titrate off anti-depressants and a hip injury which kept me from running. I tried Chiropractic in the fall, massage, time off from running. An Orthopedic visit after the new year which led to X Rays and a cortisone shot in the hip, No relief so an MRI in May and then an epidural scheduled after that.

I found myself able to run 6 miles in Vegas during the weekend of EMDR working on avoidance and feeling like "I'm not caring." I went back to childhood with an incident of a dog, Gomer, and a trauma scene of watching him get run over when I was too ADHD to get on my way and not put him back in the backyard, after he escaped for the 3rd time. This memory led to being a controlling big sister and my brother accusing me of being somewhat uncaring or something of the nature when I laughed at the way I was back then. He raised his voice accusing me of being like my father and storming out of my house, to basically not talking to me for the next 6 years…And me not knowing exactly why he was mad at me. I completed the EMDR work and decided to try and run the following day and found no major issues in my hip. Yes, a mild soreness, but not locked up with no movement like it had been for the last 8 months. While running, and racking my brain with what was going on, the song "Set Me Free' came on and the sun brightly appeared as if directed right on my body. It dawned on me that the only thing different was the EMDR this weekend and how trauma or issues are locked in our bodies and our brains. When the locked neural network was freed up, the leg must have removed the locked up muscles, also. My cardio was close to normal and my gait was almost close to what it was a year ago. It was nothing short of an EMDR miracle.

I've seen miracle after miracle in my own practice with EMDR related to body issues. One teen boy I saw for trauma at the RTC noted the enuresis and encopresis was healed after several EMDR sessions even though we weren't specifically addressing that. We were working on past trauma and anger. Note, the client brought it up and said on numerous occasions that the Eye movement therapy was making it so he was able to use the bathroom at night without accidents. Trauma is enough in and of itself, but put a bunch of traumatized male teens in an RTC wilderness camp and you get Peter

100

Pan's Lost Boys meets Lord of the Flies. It can be overwhelming for any young man, no matter what his history is. This boy was having numerous accidents for a while at the RTC, but when EMDR was started, he, himself, noticed a drastic change in the accidents. He kept saying, "I don't know how it's doing it but that eye movement thing seems to be curing me." His accidents stopped. A miracle through EMDR.

My Quest for Jungle Healing

As Americans, we tend to buy temporary moments of happiness, but when these moments end, we dive straight back into the pool of anxiety. What are we running from? Fear? Sometimes it takes stepping away from your current life to see what you have. To force yourself to travel to uncharted waters. To see how others' live, to recognize how the Ego controls you. We live our lives very selfishly. When you travel alone in a foreign country, you are forced to be an observer. To set aside the Ego and embrace the extreme anxiety to become comfortable with who you are. It's Mindfulness at the highest level by reminding yourself to live in the moment.

Robert Frost noted his thoughts on taking the path less traveled, which turned out to be a pretty good journey for him. Recently, I decided to go on my own journey and formulated a plan for healing in the jungle. I decided the journey needed to be solo to step out of my comfort zone to embrace anxiety and fear all at the same time with a focus on healing. Confused?

Let me explain. As a teen, I was one of the 25% of young females who was affected by sexual assault. I wrote about my trauma in my book, "Hyper". By my twenties, I knew I wanted to change the depression I felt, so I did what many Americans do and went to see my doctor. What do you think he did? He did what most docs do and prescribed an antidepressant. I literally tried 4 different antidepressants for probably a year before settling on the 5th one. My list included: Prozac, Effexor, Paxil, Wellbutrin before being prescribed Nefazodone, which has documentation of causing liver damage. Nice! I was on an antidepressant for 20+ years. I tried titrating off Nefazodone in my 30s, but had such horrible withdrawal symptoms (dizziness, confusion, anger, insomnia, nausea, sweating)

101

that I would go back on them each time. I wasn't depressed anymore, but my brain was so chemically altered that I needed the serotonin and dopamine to just function properly.

The fear of being on those pills for the rest of my life started to consume me in my 40s. Doing several Ironman races on antidepressants took their toll on my body. I would have hypoglycemic issues, get easily dehydrated, and had several times of being hooked up to IVs to receive fluids related to heat exhaustion. These problems, I feel, were a result of trying to do an extreme sport while on antidepressants.

Over a year ago I saw the documentary, The Sacred Science, by Nick Polizzi which sent me on the jungle journey for healing. I've also read Nick's book by the same title sharing his own journey with the jungle healing. I found out that the tribal shamans in the jungle can help a person heal many ailments. My own quest for healing was resetting my brain from antidepressants. After consulting with different companies, I found one that seemed to fit. The first assignment was to titrate successfully off the antidepressant, which under doctor's care didn't work for me in the past as they titrated me way too fast.

"We don't grow by staying comfortable", Roman says. "When we're at our edge, whether in ceremony or on an Incan trail in the darkness, we learn who is really at the wheel." Roman goes on to tell Nick, "You're going to have to learn that letting go and embracing the unknown isn't just something we do in ceremonies. Every moment of your life is sacred and loaded with subtle information that can only be witnessed by one who has clean sight. This can only be gained by letting go of who we are and the fear based anticipation of what might happen next." (Polizzi, N., 2018, The Sacred Science.)

To truly understand my irritation with psychopharmacology, you need to read "Anatomy of an Epidemic" by Robert Whitaker to grasp where I'm coming from. If you or a loved one has been affected by a long history of antidepressants or benzodiazepines this is a must read to add to your list. Luckily my brand of antidepressant was in a pill form and not a capsule. I cut my pill in small amounts at a time. It took me 7 months to successfully transition off the antidepressant.

Being "clean" from antidepressants, I was scheduled to go deep into the jungle of Peru in the summer, but I came down with a bad batch

Dana Shepard-Cardwell, M.Ed.

of bronchitis. My original jungle path included a 10-hour boat ride from Pucallpa deep into the jungle to backpack and camp for 2 weeks with the Shipibo tribe where the 85-year-old Shaman and his daughter lived. At the last minute, I backed out due to asthma-like symptoms related to my bronchitis. I had already scheduled vacation time, so I opted for a less primitive Shaman experience in the rainforest of Costa Rica.

Just arranging travel, shuttles, and taxis in a foreign country in and of itself is a day's work. It's not for the feeble-minded person. I mapped out a plan and flew into San Jose on a Friday. My 4.5-hour shuttle scheduled to Dominical beach the next day was postponed from a 9am pick up to a 2pm pick up. One must be flexible when on Costa Rica time. The shuttle driver appeared angry and drove dangerously through the rain and curvy mountains. Our drive included traversing through a 14,000-ft. mountain to get up and over to the other side where the Pacific coast of the beach town Dominical was. I arrived to Dominical stressed and highly anxious after the life-threatening ride.

Dominical was just the healing I needed. Dominical is a very small town where people from all over the world travel to surf. The town has dirt roads and looks like it is set back in the 1800s populated with hostels for affordable stay. I stayed in Cool Vibes hostel with many young world travelers. I did get a private room, while many shared dorm style rooms. The community kitchen was large and visitors could cook whatever items they purchased in town. The best Costa Rican coffee was free and plentiful. I took yoga classes, got massages on the beach, drank coconut water from fresh coconuts, and went for long walks on the rocky beach looking for heart rocks. So many life lessons were observed during my 3 days in Dominical. After the beach stay, I was on to the next journey, the rainforest.

There are things and moments out of our control, when we learn to take them as they come and focus on the "this too shall pass" to learn to be truly happy in each moment. Happiness is not bought our given to us, it's finding a way to embrace what this moment has given you. Arriving at the Florestral jungle retreat I immediately felt unwelcomed by the owner, Nicole, and her arguing children. Nicole is from Canada and her "shaman" husband is from Israel. She said very few words to me and appeared a bit passive-aggressive or deeply distracted. I arrived a day prior to the other people coming on the retreat, so perhaps I was an imposition, I'm not sure. There was a

Dana Shepard-Cardwell, M.Ed.

man, Nich, who was a regular and offered to show me to my cabana after I sat around the jungle common area for 2 hours. He took me on a tour of the compound. The toilet was a football field away from my cabana and I was told if I needed to "Pee" I should go in nature out on the grass. There was a sign in the composting toilet outhouse that read, "Poo only, no Pee in here". Yikes! I'm not sure about you, but the two usually coincide pretty close together for me. Talk about more unwelcoming signs. Then there was my cabana which had mesh wire for windows and a metal roof with 8 inches of open air space from the walls to the roof. That night a large lizard got in, mosquitoes, bugs, and the biggest moth I've ever seen, not to mention the howler monkeys that yelled all night outside my window on the tree. I thought I might be a Naked and Afraid candidate at one time in my life, but after a night in the jungle, not so much.

"You need not fear the demon hosts around you; it is most important to tame your mind within." The Hundred Thousand Songs of Milarepa.

To make a long story short, the place called Florestral, advertised as a shamanic jungle experience turned out to be a hippie hollow commune with some out of sorts characters. As a Christian, I felt the place was a little too New Age mystical for me. It was not the true tribal healing with indigenous people that I originally set out to experience. That's when I realized that Dominical was my healing. Staying at Cool Vibes hostel where people from Europe, Russia, America, U.K., etc all came to stay had its own healing vibe. The owners were so welcoming, the place was so chill, I realized that is where I got the reset I was looking for over a year ago. Plus, the yoga, the daily coconut waters, and massages all formulated a 360 reset.

My advice to you? If you have had a traumatic event in your life I recommend therapy first, prior to going directly to your doctor for medication. I did my healing in reverse order, I went to the doctor first, then did therapy, second. If I would have had EMDR therapy, something I offer in my practice, back in my 20s I know deep down I would have NEVER needed any anti-depressants. Mind you there are genetic components and times when people do need psychotropic medications, but they shouldn't be the first option. A patient should NOT have to travel around the world to be set free from the damage that 20+ years of antidepressants did.

Dana Shepard-Cardwell, M.Ed.

Traumatized individuals tend to have heightened arousal symptoms which may include: hypervigilance (always on guard), exaggerated startle responses (jumpy), problems focusing, sleep disturbances, irritability, and outbursts of anger. I certainly fit all those in my 20s and was having a hard time managing the stress of everyday life and being a single female. No matter how big or small one's trauma may be, a pill is only a Band-Aid covering up the wound. Just because a wound is camouflaged with a pill, it doesn't mean it's gone away. The subconscious mind remembers. EMDR, Eye Movement Desensitization and Reprocessing Therapy, helps allow those traumatic events to pass through adaptive information processing and heal in a therapeutic manner. Each time I took an antidepressant I essentially was covering up my wound/trauma with a Band-Aid. Once the trauma was dealt with in therapy, I got so used to the chemically altered Band-Aid, I couldn't function properly without it.

With EMDR "processing occurs when the emotional material in the limbic system is allowed to link up with the more cognitively oriented functions of the frontal lobe" (Marich, 2011). Marich points out that as humans we rely on all three brain areas to function: the reptilian area, the limbic area, and the more developed frontal lobe. "Many cognitive therapies are primarily designed to activate and work with the frontal lobe. Although talk therapy can help a person process, it is primarily a function of the frontal lobe. A person can talk all he/ she wants, but until the person can address it at the limbic level blockage traumas will likely stay stuck." EMDR helps a person move through the trauma to become unstuck and live a productive life.

If you are interested in natural alternatives to prescribed medication I recommend, *The Mood Cure* by Julia Ross (2002) a holistic approach to overcome depression, anxiety, stress, and irritability. Julia's plan can help eliminate the four most common mood imbalances.

Dana Shepard-Cardwell, M.Ed.

The massage tent where healing takes place.

What does withdrawing from antidepressants look like, again? Here's some thoughts from an article on-line by Dr. Joseph Goldberg, M.D.:

"When antidepressants that affect the brain's chemical serotonin are suddenly stopped, the body may respond with physical and emotional symptoms caused by the sudden absence of increased serotonin levels that occur while taking the antidepressant. About one in five people who take an antidepressant for six or more weeks may experience discontinuation symptoms if they suddenly stop taking the medicine.

Hardest-to-Stop Antidepressants
All depression drugs can potentially lead to discontinuation symptoms, but some are much more likely to do so than others. In fact, antidepressant labels often warn that stopping the medication too quickly may lead to bothersome symptoms. However, discontinuation symptoms are more likely with antidepressants that stay in your body for a shorter period of time, especially those that affect both serotonin and norepinephrine, such as Effexor (venlafaxine) and Cymbalta

106

Dana Shepard-Cardwell, M.Ed.

([duloxetine](#)). Other short-acting medications that affect mainly serotonin include:

- [Celexa](#) ([citalopram](#))
- [Lexapro](#) ([escitalopram](#))
- [Paxil](#) (paroxetine)
- [Zoloft](#) ([sertraline](#))

Discontinuation symptoms have also been reported in people who stop taking older types of antidepressant medications, including tricyclics and monoamine oxidase inhibitors (MAOIs).

Symptoms most often occur within three days of stopping the antidepressant. Symptoms can include:

- Anxiety
- Depression and mood swings
- Dizziness and balance problems, possibly vertigo
- Electric shock sensations
- Fatigue
- Flu-like symptoms
- Headache
- Loss of coordination
- Muscle spasms
- Nausea
- Nightmares
- Tremors
- Trouble sleeping
- Vomiting

In rare cases, antidepressant withdrawal may cause mania. Certain, older types of antidepressants called MAOIs can lead to confusion and psychotic symptoms

Your doctor will tell you how to lower your dose over a couple of days. Never try to do this on your own.
Sometimes, doctors can prescribe medicines to help with discontinuation symptoms such as nausea or insomnia. They also may advise switching from a short- to a long-acting antidepressant to ease the transition off of a medicine for depression. Discontinuation symptoms usually go away within a few weeks. But if you have extremely severe withdrawal symptoms, your doctor may recommend

Dana Shepard-Cardwell, M.Ed.

other medicines to relieve them." (WebMD Medical Reference Reviewed by Joseph Goldberg, MD on February 11, 2017.)

Makes you want to go straight to your doctor for advice on getting on antidepressants, doesn't it? (Said with sarcasm.) Why are we so ruled by these medications?

Again, I'm not against Western medicine; however, I don't think psychopharmacology is the answer for everyone and I feel doctors over prescribe all too often. Too many times diet, exercise, trauma therapy, acupuncture, and herbs are overlooked. I will note, major depression with psychosis or bipolar is most likely best treated with medication.

"Be doers of the word, and not merely hearers who deceive themselves." James 1:22 (NRSV)

Update: I just completed a week long "trip" to Rythmia Life Advancement Center and found my miracle healing. Watch the documentary on You Tube: The Reality of Truth. It is now my mission to take people there once a year to help them get their miracle. . Contact me for current dates: ***cardwellcounseling@yahoo.com***

Dana Shepard-Cardwell, M.Ed.

Meanwhile Back at the Ranch… Begin, Again.

My brother-in law, who is a hospice chaplain, noted, "Just because people know better doesn't mean they do better."

Summer at Dominguez Penitentiary:

Chris, the perp, noted feeling like he was Robert's "work wife" and yelled at and talked down at often. "When I would mess up because I'm not perfect he would yell at me, like when he would get frustrated with his wife." Chris admitted when he started using cocaine and alcohol on a regular basis, the lines got blurry as to what was real and what wasn't. Chris noted feeling like he was becoming Stacy and thought he was her. He noted his face was on some of her porn shots. It sounded like he was two people, himself and his victim. Where does this skewed thinking come from?

I asked him if he was gay and was trying to confuse himself to thinking he wasn't gay by making himself look like he was masculine by objectifying women? He thought about it and noted he felt it was more that he associated with women or wondered about problems as a woman. I wondered aloud if it was more like a gender identify issue.

He noted that it made sense. Chris shared that as a young teen he had some issues with cross dressing and then his junior year in HS, he became very depressed, wouldn't go to school, was homeschooled for a while and forgot about the sexual issues. He noted it came back up when he started drinking heavily and using cocaine.

Chris noted that he didn't tell his psychiatrist about these issues. He told me about being on Zoloft years ago and that it didn't help, but taking Depakote along with Celexa for anxiety does help. He takes his meds at the same time once a day. At times he may go for a few days without taking them if he doesn't walk to the med unit. He was encouraged not to skip his meds. He wondered if he might ever come off the meds. I described bipolar and schizophrenia like high blood pressure, it goes up and down and the best thing is to stay stable and consistent. It's like the disease of heart failure, bipolar and schizophrenia are similar with spikes up and down, the goal would be to stay stable and on the baseline to be free from symptoms and problems. He agreed that it made sense.

When I asked the perp about aggression toward one of the victims, he said he couldn't remember being aggressive on Facebook.

Dana Shepard-Cardwell, M.Ed.

He talked about seeking help through MHDD and about one therapist falling asleep on him so he didn't go back. He thought the first therapist was "Ok" but then she left. He talked about the quality of care not being good at MHDD and "One psychiatrist almost laughed at me like why are you here?" Chris shared he didn't feel supported and didn't feel like he mattered as a client at MHDD.

I feel we need more low income mental health facilities for people through private practices, so the lower socio-economic groups can get the help they need. The system continues to re-victimize people by not setting up doctors and therapists. A doctor should have all the Medicaid therapists with their expertise in their system to be able to refer a client out - prior to medication.

 A therapist should have a general tool to send the doctor if the client's level of care should be increased to include medication. In the Child Protective Services (CPS) system, children are on different levels of care and this should be the case with mental health. A mark for each area ranks a client from basic, to moderate, to specialized, to intense…. As the client increases in severity the number of targets increases, say CBT, exercise, diet regulations, vitamins, EMDR, and yes, medication. A client at a basic care level may do well with general talk therapy, but one who has had some suicidal ideations in the past may need to be at a moderate level of care with more tools used by the therapist. A client at specialized level of care may need a therapist, personal trainer, and dietician to be successful. The most intense client may need all the previous, along with medication prescribed by the psychiatrist/doctor.

Sometimes depression from situations or circumstances can be addressed with alternatives to meds such as therapy, exercise, yoga, balanced diet and working through the situational depression. Other times an antidepressant combined with therapy for a short term may be the answer. A few people who are chronically depressed may need longer terms on the meds, but not as often if appropriate therapy and medical intervention are in place.

If you recall at the beginning of the book I shared how….
a "Persuasive predator" and a "Power predator" work. The more common predator being the persuasive predator. Think about the person who "grooms" their victim. He or she takes time to invest in the victim and then zeroes in for his or her prey.

Dana Shepard-Cardwell, M.Ed.

If you happen to be a thorough reader, you should now recognize that my predator and your predator are not the people who assaulted us. That is just a tragic short event in our life. Our predators, along with a million plus others, are the psychotropic pharmaceutical companies who groom, us, their victims. Who takes advantage of us by brainwashing many doctors to prescribe a pill that at times ends up doing more harm than good.

It's time to look at the facts related to the money these companies make and the harm they do to some of the population. How is it in 30 years the population has suddenly become so mentally ill? We haven't. We have become like robots and told to take this, take that, feel better because you feel bad, etc. We have literally become like zombies either out to suck the life of someone else's blood (anger, fear, anxiety) or walk around in a coma (depression).

What happened to "This too shall pass" and just sitting with the virus that makes us ill until it passes? You shouldn't take an antibiotic for a virus that is passing through. Why should you take an antidepressant for some melancholy that will work its way through your system or something that can be helped through a few months of therapy? Why would you choose to take a pill that you may very well be taking for the rest of your life or a pill that, God forbid, gives you suicidal thoughts and one that in the end has you losing your life? Why?

After coming back from my first Costa Rican journey to healing, I was reminded of an encounter I had and trying to make meaning out of it. While in the airport at 6am ready to fly back home, I noticed a woman in Bohemian fashion attire with her three kids and husband. She was making a mild scene by fussing at her husband. As I looked closer, I noticed it was the woman from Dominical that had been in my first yoga class. At the yoga boutique, she talked up the worker about the name brand leggings she was wearing and some brand that she liked, which was sold in the boutique for $100 a piece. I was trying to be Mindful and not judge on both occasions, but at one point during class the instructor came over to align the woman in a pose. She told the instructor something about why she did the pose the way she wanted to do it and the instructor politely walked back to her spot.

In all of her theatrics, she appeared to live very LOUD and it made me think about how people choose to live their lives as a personification of a façade in looking a certain way. At the airport she

111

Dana Shepard-Cardwell, M.Ed.

appeared to demonstrate "cool vibes" with her fashion attire; however, as she tried to board the plane earlier than called, she didn't demonstrate that she was living her life off the mat like a yogi is supposed to. Does one live their life off the mat like they do on the mat?

I brought up this story to the owner of the Yoga Space, Corine, over coffee. The encounter perplexed me, since it was more than a coincidence that I would be sitting only a few feet from this woman at the airport during breakfast and that we would be on the same plane and in the same yoga class from Dominical 4.5 hours away from San Jose. The town was so small that only a handful of people were in the yoga classes. What was I supposed to gain from this encounter?

At this point in my life, I care less about how I look or present myself to others and more about being the true person God wants me to be. (However, I currently am somewhat obsessed with not looking OLD.) Am I living the life he would be proud of, am I less Ego centered? The Ego can rule or ruin our lives if we allow it.

The woman in the airport had no idea of my proximity a few feet away from her as I was taking mental notes on her situation. She didn't recognize me or pay attention to her surroundings, only that she was the center of her family and the center of her universe at that moment.

Corine asked me if there was something in that woman that reminded me of myself. That was a perfectly logical question. I thought about it and said that the woman who appeared to be in her late 30s did remind me of myself, but only back then, when I was also I in my 30s and completely self-centered.

I feel this encounter (or lack thereof) was a lesson in my journey. I need to recognize how far I have come and how many others can continue to mold and make themselves into better people over time. I believe we should forgive ourselves for past transgressions to move forward and to live each day to the fullest. I remind myself that looking a certain way and being the old Dana is who I once was, not who I am now. Each day I try to create the new and improved version of myself, but when I mess up I need to forgive myself and move on.

Dana Shepard-Cardwell, M.Ed.

I'm reminded that when I started my journey to Costa Rica I spied the woman in front of me with my favorite book, The Alchemist, by Paulo Cohelo. I love that book. I buy used copies and give it to clients. The beginning of the book starts with Santiago the Spanish shepherd boy visiting a fortune teller to find out the meaning of a dream he keeps having. In the dream a child is taking him to visit the Pyramids in Egypt. The old fortune teller tells him, "You came so that you could learn about your dreams. And the dreams are the language of God. When he speaks in our language, I can interpret what he has said. But if he speaks in the language of the soul, it is only you who can understand." (Coelho, P. 1988)

The story is about a young boy setting off on an exotic journey to find hidden treasures. However, the journey itself, the places he sees and the people he meets are the true treasures. One that ultimately brings him back home where his new treasure awaits. Have you had hidden meanings in your life that you feel need to be uncovered? If so, you are living with your eyes open. It's the Ego driven person that tends to miss these clues, as one should step away from the self to figure the clues out. The metaphors and visuals I was given during my Costa Rican journey were signs from the universe and God that we are being watched. That we need to step back, take a breath, and truly open our eyes to see beyond our own understanding.

God reminds us in Luke 10:1-20 "The harvest is great, but the workers are few. You are being sent out as Lambs against Wolves." I'm reminded of this when I look back on the time I was hurriedly trying to leave Florestral. I went from "Cool Vibes" hostel in Dominical to picking up on a sinister, evil vibe of a cult like following at Florestral with marijuana butts everywhere. The man, Ross, who took me back to Dominical for the $40 I offered him, spoke in metaphors. He talked to me about allowing myself to heal by sitting through "the medicine" to show me the way.

On our way back to Dominical, we met a Russian woman at the Farmer's market who commented on the dark energy at Florestral right now and she wasn't sure of what was going on, but that it was a healing place. Then she noticed my necklace that read, "God is Love" and told me she liked it. I told her my daughter gave it to me at a young age and I always wear it. She then looked at me and said, "Ya, and Jesus is my homeboy, right?" Something felt really wrong and awkward with her statement and the way she said it. That's when I

113

knew to trust my gut instincts and that something sinister was brewing at Florestral and getting out of there was my best option.

Luke 17:20 notes, "The Kingdom of God is not coming with signs to be observed." The problem is you and I must decipher the good and bad signs in our daily life to live the way God intended. Saint John once shared, "Let us use this world's goods as we ought, in order that we may readily receive those of the world to come." You are where you need to be right now. You have come this far, but what treasures do you hold on to?

We are all connected to God, the universe, nature, but our separateness is causing caustic decay inside us and to our planet. To help our own souls we must learn to respect and help others on their path, along with nature and our ecosystem. When we find ways to cut our umbilical cord for individualization and become united with God and mankind then we can start living and become truly free from depression, anxiety, pain, and other ailments.

To cut the cord, you must face what demons you look at inside. Too many times we chose to see the speck in someone else's eyes and refuse to look at the plank in our own eyes. I'm guilty! Secrets kill our souls. Release the secret and revive your soul. CPR for the soul will allow you to walk through the most beautiful sacred garden you have ever seen. The Garden of Eden does exist right here on earth. By removing our blinders and venturing out of our limitations life can turn into a beautiful Dove's lullaby. Have you ever heard a group of Dove's greeting the morning as the sunrises with their love songs? They have this happy, calming music that resonates inside the listener to motivate one to face the day and be content with whatever the day brings. Motivation and contentment are how we started as time babies.

Why is it most people are taking antidepressants solely from fear? Fear holds us back from the most basic things in life. Fear of failure. Fear of death. Fear of being hurt again. Fear of looking a certain way. Fear of being unhappy. Fear's possibilities are endless and we allow them to consume us. We must become vulnerable to find humility and to not be afraid of fear. There is a beautiful rainbow at the end of each storm, I promise. Life will give us storms, but you should venture out to see the rainbow. To feel the rays, to see it, to appreciate it.

Dana Shepard-Cardwell, M.Ed.

MORE SOLUTIONS for What Ails You

Dr. Van der Kolk who wrote, *The Body Keeps Score,* and is a world leader in psychiatry, addresses alternative therapies to help others overcome depression, PTSD, anxiety, eating disorders, and obsessions. He did one of the first studies with a colleague on how yoga may help heal trauma.

Dr. Michele D. Ribeiro noted in her workshop, Yoga for Trauma, that the Hedonic Principle supports the idea that material things don't make us happy, they do the opposite. She went on to share that the heart is the largest organ when we are first born. I took from her workshop that many of us need to change our views from the external world to a more internal love. We should come back to the heart and nourishing our souls.

So, what exactly is a traumatic event? It can include a physical injury (car wreck), medical diagnosis, rape, assault, robbery, mugging, emotional abuse, witnessing an accident like a wreck, experiencing or witnessing a natural disaster, combat, terrorist attacks, being a victim, being involved in civil conflict, being stalked, bullied, or experiencing stressful life events like divorce, death, homelessness, financial burdens.

Twenty percent of those who experience a traumatic event will develop symptoms of PTSD. If anywhere from 70% to the recent study of 90% of the U.S. population experiences a traumatic event at least once in their lifetime, say 220 million humans, then 20% is a large number. Research goes on to report that 1 in 3 military personnel will experience PTSD (Kessler, et al, 2005).

Flannery in Levin's work noted psychological trauma is "the state of severe fright that we experience when we are confronted with a sudden, unexpected potentially life threatening event over which we have no control, and to which we are unable to respond effectively, no matter how hard we try." Adverse life experiences like abuse, neglect, domestic violence, substance abuse in the household, mental illness in the household, divorce, or crime can lead to numerous health issues later in life. Examples of adult issues that develop due to Adverse Childhood Experiences (ACE) or Adverse Life Experiences (ALE) include: alcoholism, substance abuse, obesity, suicidal ideations,

Dana Shepard-Cardwell, M.Ed.

depression, anxiety, hallucinations, unwanted pregnancy, partner violence, sexually transmitted diseases, and diseases such as cancer and heart disease related to death before age 65.

Trauma affects our nervous system by activating the limbic area which activates our defense system. The fight, flight, or freeze is hyper-aroused and very little can be controlled at that moment. This is why yoga, mindfulness, mediation, EMDR, and taking our brain off line to deal with the unconscious can help emotions such as rage, fear, helplessness, anger, etc become a more manageable thing in our daily lives.

Our brain tends to stay in the beta wave pattern. Our goal is to slow down those waves to go from the fast beta waves to the Alpha waves which "generally happens when relaxed and focused internally" and can be referred to as the quiet readiness. From the Alpha which occurs during yoga then we can move to the Theta waves, often a creative state of the subconscious prior to falling asleep, think about a really good massage or during yoga nidra when one is about to fall asleep. The delta waves occur when we are offline per say and the brain is in "resting and regeneration" mode. I will point out there is one other wave noted as the Gamma waves where there is a burst of sharp focus (35-45hz). Our Beta waves operate at about 12-30hz. (Tarrant, 2017).

Yoga helps calm our autonomic nervous system, the vagus nerves, and the limbic system. I tell the boys at the residential treatment center over and over, "Here is your amygdala, here is your prefrontal cortex." They are asked to point to the areas on their head. I let them know with yoga and meditation, we are calming the amygdala (our area of memories that controls fear, anger, fight or flight) and allowing the brain to be able to talk to the prefrontal cortex that we are not in danger of being killed and we can train the amygdala to calm down. Many times, with the subconscious, we get stuck in the primal brain, which creates problems as the synapses don't communicate, at the moment, with the prefrontal cortex to say, "Hey brain, I'm Ok. I'm not in danger."

Van der Kolk (2014) noted "When something reminds people of a trauma from the past, their right brain reacts as if the traumatic event were happening in the present." This is an unconscious response that is why it is so important to get the appropriate help after a trauma

116

Dana Shepard-Cardwell, M.Ed.

event. Your brain is on fire; it's not your fault. Using modalities that will calm the brain on fire is what will help you feel less on fire. While the left brain remembers facts, statistics, vocabulary, the right brain stores memories of sound, touch, smell, and emotions tied to these things. It can be a voice that reminds you of your predator, a smell, a visual like a similar car, similar shoes. "Images of the past trauma activate the right hemisphere of the brain and deactivate the left" (van der Kolk, 2014).

Our minds become hijacked from the trauma or from the medications we may be prescribed, which may not be the best medication specifically for our body chemistry or mental diagnosis. Our brain cells fire electrical impulses all the time. We can learn to control some of those impulses, but others we need to sync the body with the mind so that they work together. Breath work is so important to sync our bodies and minds together and lower our brain waves to a more relaxed and controlled focused level. Electrical impulses trigger the release of neurotransmitters like serotonin, dopamine, norepinephrine, oxytocin, GABA. They are received by the dendrite of another neuron.

Addictions are so complicated. When you use a substance, it is picked up by another dendrite. So, when you stop using the substance, the dendrite is screaming, "Hey, what's up, where's my gas?" The brain starts thinking that it needs that drug. It's important to immediately replace that drug use with something else, like AcuDetox acupuncture, yoga, Nadi (alternating nose) breathing, EMDR, running, cycling, Kundalini, etc. to fill that synapsis with another neurotransmitter.

The main problem with trauma is that it remains in the body long after the event, and the brain has trouble discriminating what is the past, what is the present, and what is a real threat. (M. Ribeiro, 2019) Yoga can teach us how to control the effects of the brain to integrate the mind and the body to work together. "Energy from the brain is diffused to various parts of the body in the form of vital, healing energy. Yoga teaches the brain to be calm and passive, to accept and subdue pain, not fight it. The energy is dissipated in coping with stress and pain is diverted to healing" (Iyengar, 2008).

I use Cognitive Behavior Therapy with yoga, which supports the idea that you are what you think. We have many rooms in our minds. My

117

Dana Shepard-Cardwell, M.Ed.

daughter recently noted that she has a "mansion" going on up there because she has so many thoughts and emotions going on each hour. I noted I have a tiny home, only a few rooms I choose to live in each day. The point is, you have a choice on which rooms you choose to visit each hour inside of your mind. Your brain shouldn't rule your mind. By controlling your thoughts, you can control your brain, body, and mind. Rule your mind or it will rule you.

A technique to use when you find your mind hijacked with intense emotions is: STOP! "S" Stop what you're doing. "T" Take some deep breaths. Breathe in through your mouth, exhale through your mouth, breathe in through the nose, exhale through your nose, inhale through your nose, exhale through your mouth, and inhale through your mouth, and finally, exhale through your nose. Allow your belly to expand like a balloon as you inhale and deflate as you exhale. This has been proven in cases of anxiety, anger, fear to calm the brain and sync the body into a more calm and focused arena. After the breath work, "O" Observe what you are feeling at that moment. Lastly is "P" Proceed with your day. Use exercise daily to continue to feel your best.

Deepak Chopra reported that people who are completely sedentary are at higher risk for depression, disease, and early death. The best way to control your mind and anxiety is to get active, find a good support system, and eat healthy. I recently became a Juice Plus distributor to help people jump start their well-being without thinking about it. By having a healthy shake each morning and adding the proper nutrients in a few supplements, they can start climbing the ladder of healthy success.

Many vets with post-traumatic stress disorder are now turning to yoga to help create balance in their lives. One vet noted, "You physically learn how to calm down," he's referring to calming the fight, flight, or freeze area of the amygdala, which often gets hijacked after trauma. Cpl Jason Davey who is a vet and became a yoga instructor noted in an article by Joshua Axelrod, "When you take the time to practice twice a week, you start to look at things differently. It changes you. Your awareness level is a lot different. That's a big benefit." Another Army Ranger shared, "When I went to Ranger school they told me to lead the way. Why would men be afraid of going to a yoga class? Be one of the first men to show up to class. Don't be a wuss. Why would you be afraid of leading the way?"

Dana Shepard-Cardwell, M.Ed.

It's interesting if one looks at the 8 limbs of yoga through the Yamas and Niyamas, we find the Ahimsa addresses non-violence or do no harm to others or to one's self. The Satyas speak to being truthful in our everyday lives. The Asteya addresses not stealing, the Aparigraha practices self-restraint. The one that is even more interesting as applied to my book is the Brahmacharya which addresses us to abstain from sexual misconduct. Isn't it interesting how the Bible and the Yoga Sutras speak to many of the same things, but through different ways. One is scripture and almost in a riddle form to figure out what is being taught or said. The other has limbs. Furthermore, the Niyamas speak to observances. The Saucha addresses cleanliness. The Santosas speak to contentment. The Tapas (not wine and food) speak to austerity, these help us measure how much the body can bear pain and how much the mind can tolerate afflictions. The Svadhyaya addresses self study, and the Isvara pranidhana addresses spiritual devotion toward a higher being and to one's self. (Iyengar, 2008)

Iyengar noted that yoga brings an internal purification and invites us to go inside ourselves to work through struggles; the poses are meant to purify the mind and the body, which at times demands strength of will to bear physical pain. Think about this. God never promised a rose garden, and if he/she/it did then dont roses have thorns? Life has pain, we will go through pain. Yoga helps us bear the pain to make it manageable and less complicated. Life is a process which is evolving. The less complicated, the better in my eyes. Iyengar shared that through yoga healing comes from the premise that the body should be allowed to function as naturally as possible. Amen to that.

Just like one can create a loop or rewiring through porn addiction or other addictions, one can also rewire the brain with yoga, but in a more positive, healthy, ethically accepting way. Now which would you prefer, to be rewired to a desire that controls you, or the ability to remain calm under pressure and release endorphins to feel less pain? The endorphins released through porn are more of a high, which increases the dopamine and need for more of that reward, where yoga releases more GABA neurotransmitters which decrease symptoms of depression and anxiety. "Low levels of GABA have been linked to depression and anxiety" (K Heagberg, 2011).

Mouthy Buddha has a good YouTube video titled, "Why Porn Is Poison for Men". The cover has a seductive woman with the words

119

"Brain Damage". Another good video related to abstinence from porn on YouTube is "The Neuroscience of NoFap." Or the Bible Apps "Overcome Porn: The 40 Day Challenge".

Use some self reflection.

<u>Questions to Ask Yourself</u> (I use these in therapy)
What worries you, currently?
What do you think will happen if you do not change anything?
Are you willing and motivated to work toward a change?
How would you like things to be different?
What would you like to see different or to happen in 5 years from now?
If you could change things magically and immediately, how might things be better for you?
What are the main reasons you see for making a change?
What encourages you that you could work toward change? When in the past did you make a significant change? How did that work for you?
What strengths do you possess?
What are some common thinking errors that you have or had in the past?
Who can you turn to for support? What kind of support system do you have?
What do you do when you are stressed?
How do you remain stuck?
What encourages you that you can change?
What do you pretend or imagine?
When do you feel weak or afraid?
What do people you know have that you want? How did they get it?
What ways are you self critical?

Why aren't doctor's doing lab tests prior to prescribing psycho-pharmaceuticals?

A friend recently brought up her issue with her daughter who was admitted to a psych ward with suicidal thoughts when her antidepressant was not working. Come to find out that the girl had a thyroid issue and was suffering from hypothyroidism.

When I was training as an LPC I remember my supervisor, Carol, telling me about thyroid issues associated or mimicking depression. It

120

resonated as I too had hypothyroidism. I was already on antidepressants, so it didn't stand out too much for me; however, I do remember prior to taking Synthroid I had severe panic attacks at night and couldn't sleep. Back then I was prescribed Benzos and Ambien, which made me worse. Her words of wisdom resonated, as I too suffered from mental distress prior to taking medication for my thyroid.

I believe all candidates for psychopharmaceuticals should have bloodwork. Anemia is another one that tends to have side effects of lethargy and anxiety, along with hypoglycemia. If a person shows up to the doctor and notes feeling "blah" and lack of energy with some worry and anxiousness a doctor may immediately think it's depression related when in fact it's low iron or hypoglycemia.

Another issue for men and women in their 40's or older are hormones. A person can be experiencing a drastic change in hormones which can resemble depression. Simple lab work can expose the hormone issue. Many doctors will put a woman on anti-depressants when she is going through perimenopause or full blown menopause. Hormones would be the suggested prescription, not life altering antidepressants.

Would you give your lactose intolerant loved one a warm glass of cow's milk to help them sleep at night? I think not. I love a warm glass of milk full of tryptophan at night, but if I were allergic to milk this would not be the thing to do at night. Perhaps a glass of sleepy time tea instead? These suggestions are common sense, so why don't doctors look to see what the underlying problem is prior to prescribing?

My mission is to make the public aware of the dangers of prescribing psycho-pharmaceuticals without knowing the underlying cause a patient presents with. Depression and medical issues have a lot in common. Doctors shouldn't be throwing medication around like it's harmless candy.

According to www.webmd.com if your diet lacks essential nutrients, it can hurt your ability to concentrate. Strive for a well balanced diet with very little processed foods, fast foods, and unhealthy snack items. Eating too much or too little can affect your focus, also. Supplementing through foods like vegetables and fruits are so much

121

Dana Shepard-Cardwell, M.Ed.

better than a store bought supplement that comes in a pill. Another way to protect your brain besides a good diet Web MD noted was four simple things:

A good night's sleep, staying hydrated with water, exercising 30-45 minutes 5x a week, and meditation (can be done with yoga, quiet moving meditation). Sometimes to find true inner peace, health, and wellness, you need to step outside. I know you can do this. I believe in you. Please, get the help you need to live the life you deserve.

"There's nothing which can be more precious in you than your own relationship with your own consciousness." Yogi Bhajan

One thing to remember when "trying to meditate", when you arrive at your breath and inner silence, the monkey mind will want to take over, but wait, don't fight with the monkey. Tame your inner critic, the monkey mind, through concentration on your heart and your breathing.

Tame your mind through your breathing, notice the trees, flowers, bees, squirrels, cardinals, and nature like never before by remaining silent and listening to your breath. Travel the path less traveled by remaining quiet, listening to your breath, seeing with your eyes and soul, and leaving your head at home. It's amazing what will follow. No experience necessary, just an open mind with your thinking head at home.

So what is the solution to this pill for every type of depression pain? If you have tried all the natural resources, yet still feel depressed: Go to www.genesight.com and let yourself become the doctor and chart your own path to wellness and happiness. "By examining your DNA, a painless test lets doctors know which medications may not work for you, so you can get back to feeling like yourself again." If you need an antidepressant, then genesight.com could assist you in getting the correct depression medication.

I've recently become a Certified Mental Health Integrative Medicine Provider (CMHIMP), which takes nutritional and integrative medicine in to play to help clients heal in a natural way, not necessarily through a synthetic man-made pharmaceutical way. I love giving presentations, so email me for your next event.

Dana Shepard-Cardwell, M.Ed.

Home Work: Write your own self-leadership development plan.

Here's an example of mine from a class I took.

Fry reflects that the essence of spiritual leadership is to find a way to allow people to do what it takes intrinsically to make work rewarding. I find I have been on this path to spiritual leadership for twenty years. -leadership and self-reflection.

To travel the high road toward self-leadership one should acquire a high level of responsibility and authenticity if the leadership capacity is to be expanded upon (Manz, 2015). This reminds me of my belief that if I am to grow, I need to continue to learn more about myself, about those around me, and about the world. "Self-observation in many ways is the lifeblood of self-leadership and centers on the observation of our own behaviors to obtain information about them" (p. 135).

While further cultivating my self-leadership skills, I must increase my self-awareness which for me means looking at all cultures being spiritual, religious, and pleasant. Sadhguru notes that the first step to spirituality is to admit that I am mortal. He shares that nothing is guaranteed and that one million people die each day, which means being conscious of mortality will allow us to have a significance of just being alive or being with loved ones who are alive. He points out awareness is not about survival, it's about how alive we are. Life is brief and I must do what truly matters because too many people live their life half alive and "focus on nonsense" in their lives which does not even matter (Sadhguru, 2015).

My self-awareness includes me focusing on the very day at hand knowing that I have limited time on this earth and focusing on what I need to do now, not what I should have done in the past or what I need to do next year. To speak on the subject related to my career goals can be complex for me. I choose not to set a structured platform of where I intend to go. While I agree that setting goals and having a purpose is needed to know which direction I am to take, I feel setting timelines or deadlines only creates stress and anxiety in my life. My intrinsic goal is to be the best person I can be today, to find work that serves a purpose for my calling, and to be a caring compassionate leader for others who are hurting or in need of signs of

123

Dana Shepard-Cardwell, M.Ed.

hope and faith.

Manz points out the need for behavior focused strategies, natural rewards, and utilizing positive thought strategies. The constructive "thought strategies are based on the view that people can influence their thoughts, including the focus of mental activity and how cognitions are processed" (p. 136). Rath shares the need to find one's strengths to become more engaged in one's leadership and work environment. People are six times less likely to be engaged in their job when they are not in touch with their strengths and when their strengths are not utilized. By finding my true strengths which include strategic, activator, maximizer, ideation and woo, I believe I am to better utilize constructive thoughts as a way to stimulate personal and group excellence to transform something strong into something superb "to nurture it, refine it, and stretch it toward excellence… and to polish the pearl until it shines" (p. 137).

Spiritual leadership's purpose is to invoke vision and accordance to cultivate organizational dedication and productivity. My drive is to lead people to want to change their lives for the better, which includes the mind, body, spirit component in their personal and work life. Fry describes the universal need for people to belong and for membership. For spiritual survival, key followers need to head a calling and utilize membership. Through learning organizations followers are empowered to articulate a vision. I agree with Fry that altruistic love is key. Leaders and followers who are creating a vision need to have "genuine care concern, and appreciation for both self and others, thereby producing a sense of membership and feel understood and appreciated" (p. 695).

The concept of higher-level, self-leadership practices should reflect personal authenticity, responsibility, and expanded capacity (Manz, 2015). I agree that the center of self-leadership should be on the mind and body with a primary emphasis being focused on our behaviors and thoughts as correlated to personal effectiveness and effectiveness as a team. Furthermore, "various studies show that fitness promotes job performance" (p. 130). The authors support the findings between fitness and mental performance. My analogy would be the dementia patients I have worked with. Slower mental capacity results in slower physical reaction time and vice versa. As a clinician, I've noticed mental decline goes hand in hand with physical decline or physical decline results in mental decline. When my geriatric patients would isolate and not move around or exercise it tended to be a short period of time, like two to three months, that I witnessed their cognitive decline become impaired. I would hypothesize that a fit

124

Dana Shepard-Cardwell, M.Ed.

body is more likely to correlate to a fit mind, rather than the opposite.

To be an effective self-leader one needs self-goal setting and finding natural rewards to help increase one's motivation to exercise and eat properly (Neck & Manz, 2013). "It is easier to maintain good health through proper exercise, diet, and emotional balance than to regain it once it is lost" (Dr. Kenneth Cooper as cited by Neck & Manz, 2013, p. 138). Rath notes that "knowledge and skills, along with regular practice, are most helpful when they serve as amplifiers for your natural talents" (p. 17). External changes may happen daily around us; however, our core personality traits remain stable throughout our lives, as do our passions and interests. Working with our strengths is the key to success (Rath, 2007).

Sadhguru shares with his followers how to maintain joy and happiness regardless of external circumstances. Describing an intrinsic motivation to live with joy and become happy through altruistic love (Fry, 2003) is what I choose to focus on at this point in my life. Sadhguru shares that spirituality and happiness should not depend on the external, like the perfect job or a lot of money. He shares the emphasis is to look at pleasantness and unpleasantness and if the chances of you being pleasant 100% of the time depends on your surroundings, chances are you will not be feeling pleasant all the time. It's not possible. Pleasantness includes peace, happiness, bliss, and joy, where unpleasantness includes stress, anxiety, fear, and tension.

While I find myself at a pivotal point in my career, having recently left a well-paying job, I am searching for what I would refer to as "Dana's search for meaning". I find I must look for intrinsic value of what is important to my soul, not the external value of money, while still being conscious that I need to make money to live the life I have become accustomed to. Sadhguru shares that beliefs or assumptions are handed down by others. I find I need to fill my mind and soul with motivational and positive thoughts right now to not detour my thinking into a downward spiral while searching for work that fits my strengths (Rath, 2007). "Our body actually believes what our mind tells it" (McGonigal, 2013, as cited in How to make stress your friend, TedTalk, www.youtube.com)

Intrinsic motivation relates to a person finding pleasure and interest in an activity, such as work, for its end purpose (Fry, 2003). Generally speaking, intrinsic motivation in the work environment requires a form of self-organization for workers to feel empowered and connected to their work through a form of autonomy. The purpose of spiritual leaders is to intrinsically motivate people to find

Dana Shepard-Cardwell, M.Ed.

an intention in the workplace to feel like their work is significant and meaningful. This definition of a spiritual leader describes my life long goal to find work for myself that is significant and meaningful and work that allows me to help others find their calling and purpose, also.

Furthermore, Fry emphasizes that leaders must get in touch with their "core values and communicate them for followers through a vision, values, and personal actions" (p. 696). I believe if I am to be a worthy leader I should know what I want, first, before I am able to be a good role model for others. In my field of psycho-therapy I see many leaders who are themselves wounded and do not know what they want in their life, yet they try to lead others to a place of comfort. All this when they have not found it themselves.

Qualities of spiritual leadership include a vision, altruistic love, and hope or faith. Examples of vision include encouraging hope and faith and establishing standards of excellence. Altruistic love includes forgiveness, kindness, integrity, compassion, empathy, honesty, patience, courage, trust and loyalty, and humility. Hope or faith encompasses actions of endurance, perseverance, doing what it takes, stretching goals, and expecting a victory. I try to include qualities of spiritual leadership in my daily life as well as in my career.

In an October issue of Psychology Today, Marano writes to a reader about staying motivated while the reader is looking for employment and feeling depressed about not knowing what career is right for her. "Motivation comes from many sources, but the most important is actually doing the work (like volunteering when one is unemployed). Feeling productive is one of the pillars of the human psyche. Striving to develop competence at what you do, whatever it is, will go a long way to creating a sense of accomplishment you seek, and it could accelerate career progress on your own path, helping make up for the time you feel you've lost" (p. 22). I find reading uplifting journals or books helps me with the spiritual and motivational outlook I need at this junction in my life.

I have learned so much about the direction I want to take with the self-leadership exercises from the course of life. By looking at my strengths, I can see the value in how I present as a public speaker and how I counsel those in need. I am not the type of therapist who tries to use an Ego centered approach. I am the person-centered, mindful therapist who helps people find their strengths and to move forward and live the life they were meant to live. I accept others for their weaknesses and faults and individual differences. I

126

Dana Shepard-Cardwell, M.Ed.

have never set out to save those who are not Christians or those who are lost. I walk beside them, not in front of them.

During therapy sessions, I share a story of a yogi who would tell people not to believe him as their teacher and not to believe him because other people told them to. The yogi would say to not believe something because it was told to them in a book or a report or by authority or by tradition. And not to rely on mere logic, speculation, appearances, or inferences that something is what it is thought to be. The old yogi's message, like Jesus's message was one of acceptance of others and love for others and the power to know for yourself when something is unwholesome and wrong and to give those things up.

I share this example in talks or therapy because I believe some Christians appear hypocritical at times to those who are different, for example the amamosity toward Muslims. If I am called to share God's love to those outside my country, I must read about other cultures and other philosophies to be the person that will love and accept other nationalities, unconditionally. My Maetrix Emotional Intelligence results show I scored the highest on social-awareness. That does not surprise me as social awareness is comprised of three competencies which include empathy, organizational awareness, and being service oriented. As a victims' rights advocate, I feel these attributes define who I am as a leader.

Learning more about my strengths as an extroverted, intuitive, thinking, judging personality (ENTJ) through the Jung type descriptions has shown me that my engaged, social, adventurous personage hates to be bored, likes taking risks, and can come off narcissistic and arrogant at times, but that is alright with me as those who make a difference in the world tend to be outspoken, entrepreneurs. (Truity, 2016) Through an increase in self-awareness, I will work on not coming across as an arrogant person by being aware of this trait attributed to my personality style.

My family had never stepped out of our comfort zone to accept a Muslim student from Kyrgystan; however, as of September 2016 both were part of my daily life. I felt that God was working through me as a Christian, as a leader, and as a counselor to share his love one step at a time through our foreign exchange student, Sabrina, by allowing me to put my practices to work every day with a new and diverse addition to my family. In the past, my work with those different than myself was for an hour or two, not in my home, and not every day for nine months. I am reminded of the scripture in Acts 2:38, "Change your hearts and lives".

It befuddles me when leaders tell people to "do this" or "do

Dana Shepard-Cardwell, M.Ed.

that"; however, when I look at how they live their lives I am reminded of the messages of Jesus and Buddha to follow what my heart knows is right, love my neighbor, and steer clear of those who might veer me off course. My development plan at the moment is to find as many positive and blissful meanings in my life, because all else is "nonsense" as Sadhguru says. The fact that I woke-up today and my loved ones woke-up today makes this the best day of my life so far. I intend to do something productive with it or as miniscule as just putting a smile on my face with foreigners to brighten their day and model the Christian way of love.

My course of personality development has been determined by my biological make-up, not necessarily my life experiences (McCrae & Cost, 2008). As an extremely extroverted person with a high degree of conscientiousness I am aware that I help those who may not be as comfortable in communing with others or those who are not able to avoid conflict and may not be successful in their work or personal lives. I use positive coping tools and openness to experience with these individuals so they may lead the successful life they need and deserve.

Horowitz shares the experiences of the past 150 years suggests that positive thinking does work, but amidst different forces such as biological, natural, psychological, and even accidental. "We live under the accidents of fortune, illness, forces of nature, traumas of the past, and on the waves of relationships with others, who may possess conflicting needs and aims. These are lawful facts of life, but the mind also wields a shade of influence" (p. 294).

Conclusion

My path toward becoming a self-actualized leader continues through the courses offered at this thing called life and through my goals of being a better counselor and conflict-resolution leader by challenging unhealthy and destructive thought patterns. Goleman proposes that effective leaders all have one thing in common and that is a high degree of emotional intelligence with self-awareness being the core need. I am reminded of Romans 12:5, "In Christ we, though many, form one body, and each member belongs to all others". I first wrote about a short -term goal of knowing that happiness depends on me and no one else, nor any circumstances. To be truly happy I must know the difference between success and money and including daily hope by having something to look forward to each day, sharing with others, and making someone else happy. (Cardwell, 2016) My long term goal is to share with people ways to unify our differences and work together through peace and altruistic values, rather than creating

Dana Shepard-Cardwell, M.Ed.

conflict because of religious, individual, or cultural differences. "If my people, who are called by my name will humble themselves and pray and seek my face and turn from their wicked ways, then I will hear from Heaven, and I will forgive their sin and will heal their land" (Biblical quotes noted as sighted by biblegateway.com

My Goals Remain the Same; However,

Bhagavad Gita, reads, "Yoga is the journey of the self, through the self, to the self." When I lost my way, breath and movement led me back home to my true self.

By now you may be thinking that my perpetrator was just a hurt person hurting others, as did I. I received a second call from the FBI agents in March after meeting with three agents in February. I was told that they had in fact found altered pics of my minor daughter on his computer and they wanted us to come in to verify. My daughter was not able to make the meeting, so I was there to represent her and look at the photos in evidence. I was told there were quite a few, but they had about 10 for me to look at.

What took place was a display of disgust, outrage, sadness, and fear for my little girl. He had pictures of her in bondage. In a hostage or kidnapped way and then there were a few in leather whips and chains type pictures. He made pictures of my daughter and I having sex with him together and then another one of her peeing in a bucket. There was another of her surrounded by men with their penises standing exposed in a circle and what looked like my daughter in the middle bent down giving them oral sex and looking up. It was revolting. It stuck in my fight, flight, or freeze amygdala. Primarily the fight or flight.

My perpetrator didn't just have me in nude photos, but he went to having me with two men having sex with me in both areas, or Chris inserted himself in the fakes having sex with me. Or me and his first victim, together, or the most disturbing was with him having sex with my daughter's fake image, but with her face and then me naked in the same bed. This guy had to take it up a notch from naked posed pictures to lewd acts. Then there was the fake picture of my daughter

129

Dana Shepard-Cardwell, M.Ed.

bound by her arms and feet and gagged around her mouth on a bed. That's not a hurt person hurting people. That's a true perpetrator.

Porn has been shown to lead to human trafficking and to prove my point I'll point out a few websites which have over 43 million hits. WARNING!! This is very disturbing, but needs to be witnessed to know what pedophiles like and truly sick individuals. Also, there is a great NetFlix documentary which shows how these young girls get lassoed into the porn industry and human trafficking. Young innocent girls like your daughter, your niece, your friend's daughter, your sister. The NetFlix film is titled, "Hot Girls Wanted" and follows a teen from New Braunfels as one of the girls who are spotlighted in the amateur porn industry. The film was featured in the 2015 Sundance Film Festival. This documentary is not that disturbing, but shows how easy it is for these young girls to get manipulated and then traumatized by the porn industry.

Another, not so disturbing documentary, is Diary of a Porn Virgin found on the website, www.topdocumentaryfilms.com. A British documentary on the same site is titled, "Teen Hooked on Porn" which addresses how British teens are becoming addicts after being lured into watching porn. An older film on the same site is titled "Porndemic" (2009).
The disturbing sites that show 43 million hits includes the topic "Facial Abuse": www.xvideos.com/video "Dumb 18 year old blonde throated hard at Facial Abuse", www.facefucking.com/free "Deep Throat Chick Gets It in the Ass", "Young Latina Breaks Down After Roughface Fucking", Latinaabuse.com No ethnicities are off limits. The key words on these sites include: "abuse", "teen", "hardcore", "rough", "gagging", "deepthroat", "slapping", "brutal", "humiliation", "facial abuse", etc. It's demonic to say the least! An example of pure evil in what people get into by watching males hit, kick, choke, etc. young girls.

Back to my own case of cyberstalking which included my precious baby girl. What transpired that afternoon when I met with the FBI special agent McLoy and the local detective, Carol Twiss, on the case was a short walk in my mind from a hurt person being confused and sexually frustrated to a true psychopath, anti-social predator. A real man doesn't objectify under-age girls, only a true anti-social deviant perpetrator. I'm so glad I was able to see the true person who my perp was and not continue thinking that he was just an awkward social

130

loner who needed some mental health intervention.

No, quite the opposite, this person was truly dangerous and if he had been allowed to continue his drug induced porn, fantasy world he could have hurt someone seriously by actually acting out his fantasies. I'm so glad for the work our local law enforcement did, Captain Twiss and her detectives, and the FBI to not allow this person to walk free for quite a while. Don't be fooled by the predator, he'll use whatever means he can to tug at your heart strings and look for your empathy, but somehow he/she lacks the ability to empathize with others. Their moral compass is whacked.

I feel this was the case when I met with Chris in jail and he said all the right things to make me think he was in recovery, no, the opposite, he was just covering up (his true thoughts).

Letter from Cami to the court

Your Honorable Judge to be read to Mr. Z.

I don't want to speak to you. I don't want to see you. But I am learning that my voice is important. It wasn't the way I wanted to learn, but you gave me no choice. I was taught to forgive others wrongdoings and that God loves all. I am not sure how to do that. Since you posted pictures of me, I found myself afraid of public places for fear of seeing you or someone who saw the pictures. Imagine that, a young adult years after you did what you did afraid to go to the grocery store. It's affected my relationships, interactions, and my self-esteem. So much so, that I have sought therapy. I don't know why God made you the way you are and, frankly I don't want to know. I do think you should find out. I pray the courts will put you behind bars for the rest of your life. Why? Because I am learning in therapy, that surely I will be affected by what you did for the rest of mine.

131

Dana Shepard-Cardwell, M.Ed.

Following is a copy of my victim statement I read to the Bexar county federal court on the day of Chris's sentencing in front of Chris.

My Victim Statement in the case of Chris Z.

Anna Saltelegal, PhD in her book *Predators* shared, "There are specific techniques sex offenders and other predators use to fool people. First and most importantly is setting up a double life. Many offenders will deliberately establish themselves as the kind of person who wouldn't do that kind of thing." Dr. Salter points out, "Most child molesters are not rapists." Furthermore, "Most adults are not sexually attracted to children." "Sex with children strikes us as deeply reprehensible and utterly unappealing." However, in the past 100 years she noted psychology has twisted itself into pretzels developing different theories to answer the question, "Why do child molesters risk jail for something the rest of us wouldn't do even if it were

Regardless of why people are sexually attracted to children Salter found, "Out of every 100 offenders who would have reoffended, 60 would still reoffend even with treatment." This is like trying to cure a Type 1 Diabetic or make a person "less gay". It's not going to happen. She sums up the fact that, "This means we are a long way from curing pedophilia."

CNN reported (10/2019) that the number of US adolescents admitted to emergency rooms for injuries related to sexual abuse doubled between 2010 and 2016! (Ages 12-17) The study was published in JAMA Pediatrics and found an increase of more than 70% for child sexual abuse. More disturbing is that the study found there has been an increase in the number of young girls involved in human sex trafficking. (The study did find that it's not likely that all the increase in sexual abuse was correlated to human sex trafficking, but can account for some of the increase.)

To add insult to injury one therapist, Amy Duffy, noted in her article *Counseling Survivors of Sexual Violence*, "One thing the mental health field has shown me is that helping sometimes requires us to combat the systemic and institutionalized injustices that are prevalent in our society. I recently found myself in a counseling session with a college-aged female who was displaying feelings of hopelessness and crying profusely asking me 'Why?'. She was directly asking me

132

'why' after her sexual assault and after exercising every legal right available to her, the system was failing her. Our society and our legal system have justice gaps that are expansive. I couldn't think of an answer I could provide at that moment that would address her feelings of hopelessness."

I too was up against Mt. Everest when I, and the other victims in town, filed our complaint and statement at the local police department. The male officer told us, "Well, I don't even know if an actual crime has been committed." If we were younger, we probably would have fallen through the cracks, but we aren't. We are educated, business owners who don't take injustice lying down on our backs while someone screws us from behind, from the front, sideways, and upside down. Literally. If you saw the pictures involved in this case (100s by the way), you would know I'm not exaggerating. We took our information to the local top notch detective who happened to be female at the sheriff's department where Chris was already on probation.

What took place was a display of disgust, outrage, sadness, and fear for my little girl. He had pictures of her in bondage. In a hostage or kidnapped way and then there were a few in leather whips and chains type pictures. He made pictures of she and I having sex with him together and then one of her peeing in a bucket. There was another of her surrounded by men with their penises standing exposed in a circle and what looked like my daughter in the middle bent down giving them oral sex and looking up. It was revolting. It stuck in my fight, flight, or freeze amygdala. Primarily the fight or flight.

The most disturbing was with him having sex with my daughter's fake image, and me naked in the same bed. This guy had to take it up a notch from naked posed pictures to lewd acts. There was the fake picture of my daughter bound at her arms and feet, hog tied, and gagged around her mouth on a bed. That's not a hurt person hurting people. That's a true perpetrator.

One study found that more than 3.3 million American women were raped the first time they had sexual intercourse. The average age of rape was age 15 and the average age of the perpetrator was 6 years older than the female. Furthermore, most American women have been exposed to violence by age 24. The fight, flight, or freeze syndrome affects their amygdala for years. No one wakes up that morning

133

Dana Shepard-Cardwell, M.Ed.

knowing they will be sexually assaulted, yet it happens over and over and becomes a ground hog day for the women involved where they either turn to drugs to numb out, fight, run away from problems, or freeze with passivity in their daily lives. Young girls are not equipped to handle the stress of sexual assault and without help often go on to lead chaotic and disorganized lives.

I consider myself a strong survivor who knows how to handle criminal minds and helps those inflicted by the criminal. I was a probation officer, teacher, coach, Ironman finisher, kickboxing instructor, and now therapist; however, young girls and young women are not trained or educated to deal with people like pedophiles and master manipulators. I was lucky enough (I guess) that my sexual assault occurred at age 17 by a peer and my brain was more formed than most who become victims. I was able to work through the shame and fear that goes along with every sexual assault, but most aren't as lucky.

Turning to the subject of pornography, Gary Wilson has numerous videos on how porn consumes the male brain. His book and website www.yourbrainonporn.com shares a lot of useful information. One recent study found that pornography does lead to unethical behaviors. The results on Gary's website noted, "Consuming pornography causes individuals to be less ethical. We find that this relationship is mediated by increased moral disengagement from dehumanization of others due to viewing pornography. Combined, our results suggest that choosing to consume pornography causes individuals to behave less ethically" (Mecham,N, Lewis-Western, Wood, 2019). This study was reported in the 2019 Journal of Business Ethics.

Dr. Salter pointed out that research shows "the cornerstone of rape are distorted thinking and rape fantasies. These fantasies play an enormous role in the development of compulsive rapists." She shared, "One offender talked of his fantasy life and how he began to act out his fantasies and eventually raped not only relatives, but strangers." The convict reported, "When I was free, the age ranges that I masturbated to were around 13-17, but as I came to prison, the ages started dropping from 16 to 12 to 11 then the fantasies increased to where they didn't have any pubic hair."

Furthermore, Dr. Salter shared how alcohol and drugs release inhibitions and decreases judgement concerning sexual interests the

Dana Shepard-Cardwell, M.Ed.

person already has. She stresses, "loneliness plays a role for some. A significant percentage of child molesters do not seem to know how to connect with adults and they alleviate their loneliness through children whom they find more trusting and accepting. "

One of my clients shared her story of being groomed and assaulted by several perpetrators. She wrote to her inner child, "I remember my parents telling me I couldn't go to the game room. I lied at 12 and rode my bike and met Joe there. He was like 26 and he showed you attention. Remember how he made you feel special by being behind the counter when he worked there? You remember how excited you were to get out of school so he could make you feel special? He was nice and told me how I didn't look 12. Do you remember when you rode your bike up to his place and saw the other girl coming out and how angry you were. How you got pregnant by him and had to have an abortion at 12, only to come home late after that horrible experience to have your dad whip the shit out of you for being late. How much pain you were in and you wouldn't tell anyone." This strong woman shared that Joe introduced her to beer and cigarettes, which he would provide for her regularly. Her letter to herself was six pages long. She hooked up with another perpetrator who was in his late 20s when she was 15; he introduced her to mainlining cocaine and she became a drug addict as a teenager. She later turned to opioids which became a way to numb her mental pain. She summed up her letter to herself, "I would tell you today to tell someone, do not keep secrets, forgive that little girl, forgive your Mom and Dad for putting you last. Someone should have protected you. You were so desperate for love that for years you were with sexual predators who you thought loved you and that it was OK, but it's not, and I hope that as an adult you can help another little girl."

Since this event, saving some of the pics on my phone to show KPD as "proof" then to take to the sheriff's department as "proof", I have "memories" of those photos that pop-up on my phone, which causes distress. I was recently in the General Dollar store where a man came up to me and starting talking to me, he asked what I was doing that night and told me I was pretty. It was odd. I walked away and became afraid that he may know Chris or has seen those websites. There is something that happens weekly like that, which makes me re-victimized not knowing if someone has seen the websites and may be lurking out there. My daughter has had to start therapy this summer. His actions have cost us time, a lot of money, repetitious fear, and

Dana Shepard-Cardwell, M.Ed.

anxiety. One of the websites, which had my name and my daughter in her Tivy cheer uniform, had over 400 likes. This identified what town we live in. We live in fear of who could be stalking us.

My plea to the court, my daughter's plea, and my clients' pleas to the court is to open your eyes and recognize that this perpetrator fits the profile of a pedophile and we ask that you protect the innocent girls out there and keep him locked up for the maximum years. He committed sexual criminal acts. We do not allow those that commit criminal acts with guns or knives to have access to those weapons. Therefore, I would ask that he not have access to his weapon of choice, digital media such as computers and digital cell phones.

I also ask from the Victim's Crime funding that he be required to pay for my daughter's therapy, my podcast expense, my upcoming book, *Hijacked Minds. Protecting Yourself in a modern day Sodom and Gomorrah.* The book warns people of the dangers of pornography addiction and distinguishes the difference between hurt people who hurt others and anti-social personality disorders. We need to educate young males that pornography has dangers associated with it and we need to educate young girls about what lurks behind every Face Book post, or Snap Chat, or Instagram, or Twitter feed, and that human trafficking includes people taking videos of them in compromising positions and selling it on these porn websites. We are living in an increasingly demonic world and it's time to put our armor on to fight this spiritual warfare and start protecting the young and innocent.

Thank you,

Dana Shepard Cardwell, LPC, LCDC

As I end this journey, I'd like to point out that I'm aware that my book won't buy you happiness, but it may help you find a way to become content with life and on your own journey. Happiness is only a state of mind. We need to learn to become content in life's ups and downs to be happy. Happiness is not a constant. The only thing constant in this world is Change. Happiness is more of an outlook on life, a view from your window. It is attainable! Stop looking for it from other people or circumstances. Happiness is attainable even with creepers who lurk outside. You are welcome to hire me for personal life coaching or therapy sessions, which may lead you to your own path of happiness.

Dana Shepard-Cardwell, M.Ed.

So, what amount of time did Chris receive?

Center Point man sentenced to 38 years in federal prison for cyberstalking.

By, Louis Amestoy Dec 19, 2019

"A federal judge sentenced a Center Point man to 38 years in federal prison in a cyberstalking case involving several women from the Kerrville area.

Christopher Zamparria, 46, was sentenced Thursday morning in U.S. District Court in San Antonio by Judge Fred Briery after a jury found him guilty of downloading pictures of area women and editing their images into non-consensual pornographic scenes he shared on websites.

One of the women, Dana Cardwell, provided a victim's statement during the hearing. Cardwell, along with her teenage daughter, had their images placed on hundreds of pornographic images.

"What took place was a display of disgust, outrage, sadness, and fear for my little girl," Cardwell read in court. "He had pictures of her in bondage."

The sentencing ends a nearly three-year ordeal for the victims, but this is not the first time that Zamparria has been caught altering images he's obtained from the social media accounts of local women. In 2013, he was sentenced to probation for creating nude images of former Kerrville City Councilwoman Stacie Keeble.

Assistant U.S. Attorney Bettina Richardson said the outcome of the case should be a wakeup call to people about how they distribute photographs and video online and via social media.

"This exemplifies the danger of how much we make available when it comes to our personal information," Richardson said. "Once someone has that information there's not stopping it.

137

Dana Shepard-Cardwell, M.Ed.

"I don't want this to seem like we're blaming the victims here, but when we put images out there we are subject to whatever someone wants to do with them."

The case ended up in the federal courts because cyberstalking and child pornography are federal crimes. Cardwell, who is friends with Keeble and knew Zamparria prior to his arrest, was alerted to the fake images in the summer of 2017. She initially took the issue to Kerrville Police Department, before it ended up with Kerr County Sheriff's Capt. Carol Twiss.

The investigation ultimately revealed that Zamparria had altered the images of porn by removing the heads from images and replacing them with local women, including Cardwell's daughter who also provided a victim's statement. At least one other woman spoke during the sentencing that Zamparria had harmed her and made her feel unsafe.

Zamparria's federal public defender Kurt May did not return a phone call seeking comment.

While Cardwell credit's Twiss' diligence in the matter, the FBI did much of the work to investigate the images that led to Zamparria's prosecution.

"Digital forensics is very complicated," Richardson said. "It requires tools and resources that local law enforcement doesn't have. (Local law enforcement) knew how to handle it correctly by calling the FBI. The FBI has the resources and tools to handle this."

Cases like Zamparria's have taken on a sense of urgency for law enforcement due to easy access to software to make the images, and a worldwide network to distribute pornographic content. Studies have shown that this non-consensual porn is the primary use for these fake images.

"Another key trend we identified is the prominence of non-consensual deepfake pornography, which accounted for 96% of the total deepfake videos online," wrote Giorgio Patrini, the CEO of cybersecurity firm Deeptrace, which is tracking and trying to combat the rise of fake images and videos across the internet. "We also found that the top four websites

Dana Shepard-Cardwell, M.Ed.

dedicated to deepfake pornography received more than 134 million views on videos targeting hundreds of female celebrities worldwide. This significant viewership demonstrates a market for websites creating and hosting deepfake pornography, a trend that will continue to grow unless decisive action is taken.""

The judge slammed Chris! Gave him 38 years and 4 months. One of the longest sentences given to this date related to deep fakes, cyberstalking, and to make an example of the dangers related to these types of crimes. The judge threw the book at him, well not literally.

The judge noted Chris would have plenty of time for his prison ministry as Chris tried to say he found God and is a Christian now. Chris' attorney also tried to use the issue of being bipolar and not medicated as a reason for his crimes. Luckily, the judge didn't buy that either. Thank goodness. Federal crimes require prisoners to serve 80% of their time before coming up for parole, so Chris will serve at least 30 years before he can come before the parole board. That will make him 76 by then. I kind of felt sorry for the S.O.B..

Red Flags for Pornography or drug addictions:
Continue to use despite adverse consequences. Preoccupation. Problems with family, work, education, or legal system. Tolerance, needing more or different forms. Deterioration of relationships (lies, excuses, letting people down). Withdrawal, social isolation. Denial (rationalizing that it's not really a problem).

Those with an addiction problem with pornography continue to use despite bad things happening in their lives related to the above. Addiction usually has the person being less honest with red flags or unusual excuses. The person may hurt family members, disappoint people and cause problems for those around them. The people around them become uncomfortable because of the addict's unpredictable behaviors and fear of confrontation. People want to believe the addict's lies or excuses. The dishonesty causes conflict in all areas of the addicts life and those associated with the addict. Denial is used as the addicts defense mechanism. Denial is about fooling those around the addict and the addict themselves. It's easier for them to lie to themselves and others in their minds. The addict does not see reality while using. They are looking

Dana Shepard-Cardwell, M.Ed.

through the rose colored glasses of denial, while those around them see dirt, muck, and poo brewing in their vicinity. They become full of SHIT in a sense and it's easy to smell, but those around them can't figure out where it's coming from. Ie not knowing what their addiction may be: porn, drugs, alcohol, etc. It's hard to address with teens because often they have a "I don't care attitude" and "You don't know what you're talking about" because most adults are stupid in their eyes and they think there's not a problem. Even when they aren't getting out of their room, not showering, showing a decrease in schoolwork, are becoming more irritable, being sarcastic, and showing overall irrational behaviors.

Everyone processes trauma differently. As my incident came to closure, I noticed how over the past two years since "the drama" first started, how distracted and preoccupied I'd become. Add some anxiety, rushing, and OCD to that mix. Some people say, "If God really loved me he wouldn't have let this happen to me." As I mentioned previously, God gave us free will, meaning some people get messed up in the wrong sort of stuff.

Isaiah 53:5 "He was pierced of our transgressions. He was crushed of our iniquities, by his wounds we are healed." My mind became fixed on playing God per say. That's a problem and my OCD mindset of making sure I educate people on the dangers of porn and the OCD of getting my perp the most time allowable took me away from God. I used to read my daily devotional, but it was hard to concentrate and be with God. I became less grounded and less available for the present situation. I lived for the future: finishing this certification, taking that class, writing this book, getting the most time sentenced, writing the victim statement, starting a podcast. And then guess what?

I got what I asked for. More so. Way more. Then came the feelings of guilt. Remorse. Feeling sorry for him. There was less OCD of what I thought needed to be done, but more looking at change in my life. From my private practice to completing this book to presentations, to confusion. Deep confusion. Why do I feel sorry or remorse for the perpetrator? He looked so feeble in court. And now he will live the majority of the rest of his adult mid-life behind bars. I should be able to slow down and enjoy now.

140

One of my clients, about to be 30, was struggling with getting older. I told her the 20s were crazy making, half child, half adult. But the 30s are about actually becoming an adult. Settling down, setting one's principles that you learned you had in your 20s. She noted she gave her mother a lot of grief in her early 20s and how she was promiscuous. She agreed that now that she has a child of her own she wants to work on finding the right relationship, moving on from her baby daddy and deciding what direction her career needed to go. She has her whole life in front of her, but my perp will never have a child of his own by the time he gets out. No "do-overs" like my client.

Isaiah 56:1-2 "This is what the Lord says, Maintain justice and do what is right, for my salvation is close at hand and righteousness will soon be revealed. Blessed is the one who does this, the person who holds to it fast, who keeps the Sabbath without desecrating it and keeps their hands from doing any evil."

What wake-up call have you had or what do you need to wake-up to or from? Set goals, work for them, but take baby steps. Change won't happen overnight. Change requires motivation first, then setting the steps in place to move toward a transformation.

Colossians 1:21-23 "Once you were alienated from God and were enemies in your minds because of your evil behavior. But now he has reconciled you by Christ's physical body through death to present you holy in his sight, without blemish and free from accusation. If you continue in your faith, establish firm and don't move from the hope held out in the gospel."

I admit that Evil jaded me. Negative people have affected me. It's taken me away from God. And this is just what the devil wanted. Don't you agree? What has the devil succeeded to do in your own life? What are you preoccupied with? Food, work, Facebook, Instagram, a SnapChat streak, drugs, alcohol, porn, affairs, divorce, grief, loss? My message now is to share with others who may be struggling, just like I was. God doesn't want us to isolate and do this thing called life alone. Isolation leads to more anxiety, more depression, more distress, more dis-ease. Find a support system.

Dana Shepard-Cardwell, M.Ed.

Evil tends to preoccupy us. I previously mentioned spiritual warfare. What keeps you from God? What keeps you from attending to your Mind, Body, and Soul? Our bodies should be God's temple. Our minds should be focused more on him and on what is good. We should be taking care of our temple by eating the right foods, exercising, taking in nature. Taking care of our soul means slowing down and meditation on God's word, being Mindful of our day by slowing down.

How is God using you? Have you considered that your adversities could be a medium God is calling you to speak out on? Financial debt, harassment, assault, death of a loved one, cancer, bullying, addiction, injustice, social media, divorce, obesity, etc? Once we flush the secrets and unclog the toilet from trying to hide our secrets, it's amazing how free we become. Yes, it's hard at first, coming clean. But once the toilet's unclogged, you can clean up the mess, and even wash your hands in that bowl.

Years ago people misunderstood Jesus. Isn't that the case with you? If you're coming clean, doing right, helping others, having a pure heart and soul, why does it matter what other people think? Not everyone will like you and me. Not everyone will we please. Set those who work against you aside, be polite, but move on. Bite your tongue in their presence or when their name comes up and be you. If you have already taken the steps to change for the positive other people will recognize your hard work, especially God. Some people will not recognize your progress, but that's OK.

Paul was blinded by God's light. Allow God's light to shine in on you, look for it, it's there, I promise. We get weighed down with too many words and too much preaching. The Bible shows us to have Faith. Lean In. Experience God. Help others and lead by example, not by preaching or words. Rhetoric is killing our communities.

Social media like Facebook/SnapChat/Instagram is killing young females. New studies have found girls ages 12-19 who spend time regularly on social media suffered from depression and/or eating disorders. Facebook has made it easier for girls to spend more time criticizing themselves by thinking everyone else is happier or looks better than they do. To add to this, these girls are more impressionable and

Dana Shepard-Cardwell, M.Ed.

more likely to hook up with a stranger who is paying attention to them online. This is how many perpetrators find their victims.

While social media is killing our young females, pornography is killing young men's chances of a successful marriage by warping their minds related to what they think sex should look like. Porn falsely portrays how to treat a woman or that women like to have sex while being slapped, hit, or choked. Some young men develop porn induced erectile dysfunction, which further limits their chances of a happy relationship. Teens are frequently unaware of the risks that porn addiction causes. If there are no consequences then the young person has no reason to stop. The first step to take is to confront Denial. Don't turn a blind eye to the Red Flags or your friend, son, husband, brother, co-worker, partner may end up with 38 years like Chris.

Furthermore, drugs are killing our loved ones. Most drug and alcohol treatment centers will tell you that drugs act on the brain which cause social controls to be loosened and there is an increase in aggressive and sexual behavior. Alcohol is destroying our lives. Fake Food is causing diabetes, cancer, addictions, and yes, it's killing us. How many people overeat broccoli, cauliflower, or peas? No, those are God made foods and are not addicting like ice cream, sodas, french fries, donuts, chips, candy bars, Frappes, Lattes with flavor. It's the man-made, Devil made, foods that are addicting. If it comes from your own garden or your own ranch, it's probably good for you. How can we take back our lives and live the life God wants us to live? Can you see how Sodom and Gomorrah are here, now?

In church today, a few weeks after the sentencing, we read the Lord's Prayer, which asks us to "forgive us our trespasses as we forgive those who trespass against us" (those who have hurt us). I was reminded that I had forgiven Chris for his actions and the deep sorrow I had for him. (Not so much for the guy who raped me as a teen, but more for Chris, the stalker, and his addictions.) Chris's addiction to pornography and drugs led to having no real life in his adult years. No chance for having kids, a good job, family time, and living the American dream with a clean slate. No, he lived his 30s with his parents while using drugs and pornography, and now he's living his 40s in the pen and won't get out until his 70s. What chance does he have of having a child or getting a good job? Ok, so

Dana Shepard-Cardwell, M.Ed.

maybe he'll get married, but he'll be an old groom, and the other two are not likely.

My Beautiful Cami's letter to herself after being assaulted, used, feeling down and alone, etc.

To Myself (part 3)

Hi baby. I just wanted to apologize and admit some things. I love you. And I know you blame yourself for all the times you couldn't say no. I know you want to say that you were the reason it happened, that it was easier to say yes, or nothing at all, because you were afraid. You were afraid that if you said no, they wouldn't want you anymore, or if you said no, they would force you and you'd have to go through another assault situation. But it's okay baby, I don't blame you. It's okay to be afraid, it's okay to admit you've been through a lot. I don't hate you. I think it's time to forgive yourself. You don't need to carry the blame anymore, give it to God, let him take it. If you can forgive those boys that put you through it, forgive yourself for allowing it. We can grow from this. Allow the pain and guilt to leave your heart, you've carried it enough. God is changing you, He is working in your heart. I know it's hard for you to trust boys because deep down you don't even know if you can trust yourself anymore. Well, you know who you can always trust, God. And He has your hand, and heart, and He has, and is, working and changing you. So as you start allowing yourself to trust in me again, know it's okay because as long as you are trusting God first, you can trust that we are becoming trustworthy. But before I end this, I just want you to know… stop blaming yourself. You went for assholes, so what, *they* are the ones that took advantage of you, *they* are the ones that worked their way into your pants, you were just another one of their victims. Forgive yourself. God did.

As Dr. Bessel van der Kolk noted, "The thing that gets most messed up with trauma is self-experience and the ability to meaningfully connect with one's self and with others. The nervous system gets overwhelmed, the body gets so aroused and reactive that the calm and relaxed state needed for healing and connection is difficult to imagine, let alone reach." This is why some of us, the doctor himself, recommend yoga,

144

mindfulness, EMDR and meditation to heal the trauma as it has to be experienced on the subconscious level and the body has to work through the stress release to move forward and leave the trauma behind. Through a challenging yoga practice the body and mind become stronger, more balanced and they connect. Once this falls into place the subconscious mind is able to relax and recognize that peace is part of the new plan.

We are all sinners. Unlike Chris, the beauty is that we can start over, again, with a clean slate. Don't feel unworthy, anymore. Write down 10 positive words that describe you, right now, and 10 goals you hope to accomplish. Some goals this month, some this year, and some in the future. Get on your way, you are strong. You Are Enough!

I'm reminded of my favorite saying by a wise doctor. "Be who you are and say what you feel because those who mind don't matter and those who matter don't mind." (Dr. Suess) Get on your way, you have places to go and people to see.

The moral of this hijacked minds journey? We can only change ourselves, not others. I choose to move forward and use disturbances in my life as lessons learned. I choose to focus on the good in people, not those who won't or choose not to change. I stay away from toxic people for the most part. I move forward in harmony with those who will change and learn. Life is great. ***Peace be with you & take back your hijacked mind, before it's too late!***

Contact me, Dana Cardwell, at www.hijackedminds.org
Look for our healing retreats at www.healingelements.org
Don't miss my new Podcast, Hijacked Minds.
And my Juice Plus website to get healthy.
www.dc91377.juiceplus.com It only takes a few capsules daily to get healthy and feel blissful.

Here are some mental health apps and downloads related to Mindfulness for your journey to happiness.

www.freemindfulness.org
Headspace is a calming app to help address many issues.
The Calm app is another app to help one sleep and rest.

145

Dana Shepard-Cardwell, M.Ed.

Happify is an app for stress and worry.
Colorfy is an app related to coloring therapy for adults.
Mental Health and You (MHU) is a mobile app designed to help you learn about mental health disorders.
Down Dog, My favorite slow flow yoga app
Medscape has medical topics
Bellabee sells an affordable device for anxiety, focus, sleep
Song on drugs: "If I didn't have a brain" Garth Bacon

<u>You Tube inspirational videos to check out:</u>
"Just Breathe" by Julie Bayer Salzman
Bessell van der Kolk: Overcome Trauma with Yoga
Overcomer Animated Short: Hannah Grace
University of Texas at Austin 2014 Commencement
The Reality of Truth (2017 Ayahuasca Documentary)
I Am A Victim of Sexual Assault. MyLifeAsEva
ABC World News-Meditation
Meditation 101 – Learn How to Meditation
How Mindfulness Empowers Us : Happify
Why Mindfulness is a Superpower: Happify
DESENSITIZED: Media Violence and Children
Your Brain Vs Porn/ BuzzFeed
Brene Brown on Empathy
The Correct Way to Breathe In/ Tech Insider
Got Negative Thoughts? Meet Coach for Mindfulness
What Role Does Trauma Play in Addiction?
Trauma and EMDR
The Teenage Brain on Porn/ ABC News Nightline
I'm Truly Sorry Short Bullying Movie
Why Porn Changes the Brain/ What I've Learned
Why Exercise is so underrated/ What I've learned
Jessica's Story My life as a porn star
Porn Induced Erectile Dysfunction (PIED)
The No. 1 Habit Billionaires Run Daily
Brain 101/ National Geographic
The Science of Pornography Addiction (AsapScience)
How to Remain Calm with People/ The School of Life
The Three Main Parts of Your Brain by Dr. Russ Harris
Why the teenage brain has an evolutionary advantage
Anger Management Techniques/ Watchwellcast
E60: The RA Dickey Story (on male sexual assault)
Your Brain on Porn: How Internet Porn/ BodyWisdom

Dana Shepard-Cardwell, M.Ed.

My Story/ Elizabeth Smart/ TEDx Talks
What are sexually addictive behaviors?
Signs you could be a sex addict/ Katie Couric
Smashing ANTs Kid Empowerment, Nancy Sheain
The Truth About Sadness in Inside Out/ The Theorizer
I Jumped Off The Golden Gate Bridge (Suicide ideations)
How to Conquer Your Mind and Embrace the Suck (lang)
First Impressions: Exposure to Violence
Through Our Eyes: Children, Violence, and Trauma
Listen to Me – Short Film (Windstruck Production)
Stress, Portrait of a Killer, Robert Sapolsky
The Guest House – Rumi
Effects of Media Violence on Children/ Ayumi Tomioka
Evan/ Sandy Hook Promise (on school violence, guns)
DIY Calming Glitter Jar (MsXialin)
How Anger Goes Out of Control
All Emotions have purpose with Rumi/ Gozenonline
Quicksand/ Robot Chicken/ Adult Swim
The Science of Yoga, Infonostica (Part 1, 2, 3, 4, 5, 6)
10 Traits of a Psychopath. Psych2Go
Personality Disorders: Crash Course Psychology
Calm Down and Release the Amygdala
The Most Important lesson from 83,000 brain scans
Everything you think you know about addiction is wrong
The Price of Shame/ Monica Lewinsky
A Japanese Method to Relax in 5 minutes
The Giving Tree
Hours from Death: Anorexia Sufferer's Incredible
We Are Alive: Kent Gustavson
Harvard Scientist Explains What Porn Does to your brain
A letter from a sex addict in prison by Linda Hatch
Satan's Final Frontier: The Sex Industry
Porn Induced ED: The #1 Sign You Have It
Murder, Mayhem, and Meditation (48:59 minutes)
What a 15 year old meth addict taught me about life
Adam Brown – Inspirational Navy Seal
KARK News 4 Report on the life of Adam Brown
Mindfulness Animated in 3 minutes
3 Ways to Deal with that feeling of Emptiness

Dana Shepard-Cardwell, M.Ed.

References

Bible quotes from Chronicles and Romans cited by
http://www.biblegateway.com/passage/2+Chronicle+7%3A1
4&version=NIV&interface=amp

Cardwell, D. (9/2016). Life and career goals. LEAD 714.W5 Self-
Assessment in Leadership. Abilene Christian University.

Cardwell, D. (2015). Hyper. Amazon Books.

Costa, P.T. Jr and McCrae, R.R. (2008). The five-factor theory of
personality. In O. John, R. Robins, L. Pervin (Eds.),
Handbook of personality: Theory and research (3rd ed). New
York, NY: Guilford Press.

Fry, J. (Nov. 5, 2014). The purpose of spiritual leadership. Retrieved
from https://www.youtube.com/watch?v=2ruUmuSTWfU

Fry, L. W. (2003). Toward a theory of spiritual leadership. The
Leadership Quarterly, 14(6), 693–727.

Goleman, D. (2004). What makes a leader? Harvard Business
Review, 82(1), 82-91.

Horowitz, M. (2014). One simple idea. New York, NY: Skyhorse
Publishing.

Manz, Charles, C. (2015). Taking the self-leadership high road:
Smooth surface or potholes ahead? The Academy of
Management Perspectives, 29(1), 132-151.

Marano, H. (2016). Behind my peers. Psychology Today, 49(5), 22.

McGonigal, K. (2013, June). How to make stress your friend
(TedTalks). Retrieved from http://www.youtube.com.

Maetrix Emotional Intelligence Test (2016, September). The
meatrix EI test results (MEIT Version 1.0). Retrieved from
http://www.maetrix.com.au/cgi-bin/eiscore.pl.

Dana Shepard-Cardwell, M.Ed.

Neck, C. P., & Manz, C. C. (2013). Mastering self-leadership:
    Empowering yourself for personal excellence (6th ed.).
    Upper Saddle River, NJ: Pearson Education, Inc.

Neck, C. P., & Milliman, J. F. (1994). Thought self-leadership:
    Finding spiritual fulfilment in organizational life. Journal of
    Managerial Psychology, 9(6), 9–16.

Rath, T. (2007). StrengthsFinder 2.0. New York, NY: Gallup Press.

Van der Kolk, Bessel (2014). The Body Keeps the Score.
    New York, NY. Penguin Books.

Sadhguru (May 29, 2015) The first step in spirituality. Retrieved
    from https://www.youtube.com/watch?v=AoBp9jM8fZo

Truity (2016). Personality Types: ENTJ. Retrieved from
    http://www.truity.com/personality-type/ENTJ

Dana Shepard-Cardwell, M.Ed.

Body
Mind
headaches
frequent infections
taut muscles
muscular twitches
fatigue
skin irritations
breathlessness
worrying
muddled thinking
impaired judgement
nightmares
indecisions
negativity
hasty decisions
Stress
loss of confidence
more fussy
irritability
depression
apathy
alienation
apprehension
accident prone
loss of appetite
loss of sex drive
drinking more
insomnia
restlessness
smoking more
Emotions
Behavior

NOTES:

150